MW01294081

The Handbook for Starting a Business as a Natural Health Consultant:

A Guide for the Professional.

By Kay K. Larson, Ph.D.

Praises for *The Handbook for Starting a Business as a Natural Health Consultant: A Guide for the Professional*:

"I read Kay Larson's book and found it to be the best and most informative book I have read on building a natural health practice! I consider it to be my practice bible. I highly recommend it. It has already opened doors for me!"
-Cindy H.

"I downloaded Dr. Larson's book last night onto my kindle and was up for hours. I couldn't put it down! Great information. I'm sure I'll read it many times over and over. Thank you for sharing such great information with all of us! It is extremely helpful in understanding the business from start to finish. Great book!"
- Rose M.

"Okay folks I just finished the book and for the record I am not a salesman promoting it. I am a very critical person when it comes to the intent of book writers/publishers (being one myself). Some people publish because they have to (professors), some publish to make themselves bigger than they are (fame grabbers) and others publish to get the word out and educate (Dr. Larson).I have purchased many books to help me along in current business, but nothing like this. This book is an easy and VERY informative read. Dr. Larson "tells it like it is" and keeps the reader and future business owner in mind to get you started right away on a path to success. It's worth the money I paid for it. It is a big part of my business development and company expansion."
-James B.

"Dr. Larson did a superb job with this book! I found it to be very helpful and educational. As a student in the holistic health field, I had many questions regarding my future business and/or career. Her book answered those questions and more! I highly recommend this book to anyone who is considering working in the field of natural health."
-Jen E.

"I liked the book very much. No, that's not right. I LOVED the book. I liked the straightforwardness, honesty, and the " in your face" facts. It was refreshing, and I'd be proud to offer it to the VoiceBio practitioners as well as the thousands on my Information4U newsgroup!
-KThompson

"An excellent resource for a new or established holistic health consultant. I use it now and will refer to it in the future.
-Kim T.

Revised September, 2011

ISBN 978-0-557-06086-3

Dedication

To all Natural Healers new to the field, may this help you begin your journey and:

To Robert, *you were there all the time.*

Table of Contents

Introduction-Why America Needs You

So, you've decided to enter the growing field of natural health. This is the book I wish I'd had when I was first starting out. I would have paid dearly to learn the "to do's and the "what *not* to do's" from someone who had done it. Now you have it. You don't have to reinvent the wheel. You can learn from someone else's experience. And trust me, it will make your career go much smoother in the beginning!

You may find this book a little edgy. That's because I'm going to tell you the truth. I'm going to tell you what it takes to make it in business and I'm not going to sugarcoat it. And the first thing I'm going to tell you is that it is *not* easy. Yes, natural health is a growing field, but we still have a long way to go. No matter. The United States still needs you, desperately. If you for any reason doubt that, take a jaunt to the local mall sometime and spend some time watching the people there. Take a good look at their physiques, faces and eyes. If they're teenagers, you'll see pimply, pallid faces and vacant stares shuffling around with drooping shoulders. If they're adults you'll see graying hair, thinning hair, no hair, glasses, glassy eyes, double chins, potbellies, puffy faces, wrinkled faces, wrinkled foreheads, bad teeth, and bad coloring and sometimes 30-40 pounds of extra weight. If they're elderly, you'll see liver spots, false teeth, no teeth, cloudy eyes, stooped shoulders, canes, wheelchairs and walkers. If they're children, you'll see fidgety, restless, ants-in-the-pants boys and girls that are so pumped up on sugar, they are unable to sit still for a second. Also note that many of these kids are already fat, just like their parents, older brothers and sisters.

Next, please observe that many of these people, as they aimlessly mill about spending money needlessly, are holding things in their hands. Things like big pretzels with salt and mustard, ice cream cones, 20-ounce sodas, chocolate chip cookies, popcorn, hot dogs, and coffee concoctions with three-word names. If it's lunchtime, stroll on down to the food court. Look at the long lines at the pizza places, burger joints, and taco stands. But, before you go home, pop into the local drug store. Notice the long lines at the pharmacy department and observe the expressions on the faces on those waiting in them. Not too many smiles there, wouldn't you say? With the cost of medical insurance and the way some of these folks are feeling, I wouldn't be smiling either. As you leave, think about the overall demeanor of the people you've just observed. Do they seem content? Forget the ones in the pharmacy, how about the ones who have the means and mobility to be out shopping. Do *they* seem happy? Oh, and on the drive home, take care that you're not a victim of road rage.

Unfortunately, this description could fit any shopping mall in America at any time. It is not the exception; it is the norm. There is a spiritual and physical malaise affecting the entire nation. Very few people look well and even less seem content. We've become soft, fat, depressed, restless and sick. Our lives are out of balance and off-kilter with skewed values and priorities. The majority of us who live in America suffer in some way, either emotionally or physically. We're on Prozac and St. John's Wort. We take antacids and painkillers by the carloads. Our children are on Ritalin. And despite of all this, we are told that this is the healthiest, happiest time in history and we are living longer than ever before. *But our experience does not validate that claim.* People live in fear in America; psychosis abounds. Some are afraid to live. Some are afraid to die. Some are afraid of an economic disaster. Some are afraid to commit, yet afraid to be alone. Some are afraid to succeed, yet don't want to fail. Some are afraid of terrorists and some are afraid of the government. But most of all, we're afraid of our own physical futures, afraid that we, too, will come down with a terrible disease leading to a slow and painful death, as so many of our friends and relatives already have.

It seems almost a certainty that if we live long enough, we'll develop one of the Big Three — heart disease, cancer or diabetes. And if that doesn't do it, there's always Alzheimer's to worry about. Chances are that our last years will be spent languishing with aches and pains, surrounded with an assortment of drugs. If we end up in the hospital — which is very likely — we'll have doctors and nurses we don't know, hovering over us, not caring one way or the other whether we live or die. No one dies of natural causes at home anymore; we all know that.

Officially, 1951 was the last year anyone in the US died of old age, and the classification was eliminated as a cause on death certificates. No wonder we're scared.

Since 1900, more money has been spent and more knowledge gained on health and disease than in all of history combined. America is the richest nation in the world and *supposedly* possesses the best health care of any nation. We have the best doctor-patient ratio in the world: 1 to 8. Yet, compared to countries where the food supply is adequate, we are the sickest. Today cancer is estimated to affect 1 out of 2 people. In 1985, it was 1 out of 3. In 1909, it was 1 out of 33. In 2009, leukemia is the number one killer of children; although 80 years ago it was virtually unknown.

Heart disease is still the number one killer of Americans, but cancer is poised to take that position. Maybe because the medical community has become quite proficient in prolonging the lives of heart attack victims so they can develop cancer later. Diabetes is the seventh largest cause of death in adults. In 1900, it was the 27th leading cause of death. In 1975, researcher William Dufty stated that virtually all of America is pre-diabetic.[1] Yet, insulin as a medical treatment was discovered in 1923!

It is now estimated that over 70% of adults over 40 have a chronic degenerative condition. In 1900, that number was only 20%. Young people are now developing conditions that only a

---

[1] William Dufty, *Sugar Blues*, 1975

short time ago were associated with advanced age. Gall bladder surgery among twenty year olds is becoming commonplace. So is arthritis. Sixty six percent of adults are overweight and 32 % are flat-out obese.

Children are suffering, too. In addition to the rise in chronic diseases associated with childhood such as diabetes type I, adult-associated problems such as heart disease have been diagnosed in children as young as eight. They are also being afflicted with physical situations that they are in no way able to handle, such as girls as young as six years old menstruating. Behavioral problems and mental illness have skyrocketed. Who could doubt this when murderous children and teenagers are all over the news?

What is happening? Why is our physical and emotional health declining so dramatically? First, let us take a hard look at the people and organizations we are entrusting as *the* final authorities concerning health and disease and let us examine our attitudes toward them. That may give us some idea as to why we're in this predicament.

Most of us in the USA put medical doctors on a pedestal, holding them in the highest esteem. We've been taught to believe that their judgment is above reproach. We want to believe that they are honest, committed, well equipped and learned concerning our health. After all, they've spent years and years studying difficult and complex concepts, quite often at great personal and financial sacrifice. They've got the education and the expensive equipment. They prescribe medicines, vaccines, and perform operations that have saved millions of lives (or so everyone believes). So when we visit them for a problem and they tell us what to do, we would never think of questioning them ... because they are the experts on health. But, are they worthy of such blind devotion? And more importantly, do they have what it really takes to guide us into what we want, which is optimal health? Can they tell us what to do so we can live our lives with freedom, dignity and grace?

To answer these questions we must first define the word "health." Health is when the cells in the body are functioning at optimum capacity, carrying out the functions they were designed to do. But this is *not* how the current medical community defines it. A person can be 50 pounds over weight and smoke like a chimney, but as long as that he is asymptomatic and registers in the "normal range" on the standard tests, a doctor will send him home and tell him all is well. *That's what the medical model of health is: No symptoms, normal test results.* A friend of mine had an uncle who went in for a complete physical. The doctor did the tests, said he was fine and gave him a clean bill of health. Four days later, he died from a massive heart attack. How could *that* have happened? Obviously, this man was *not* healthy!

Let's also define the word "cure." Orthodox medicine defines it as something that eradicates *symptoms*. You have a headache, take an aspirin; you have a malignancy, remove the tumor; you have an infection, take an antibiotic. But, aren't headaches, tumors and infections just symptoms of a deeper problem? Therefore, aspirin, tumor removal and bacteria-killers aren't cures at all (even though at times they may be desirable and necessary). The true definition of a "cure" is a catalyst that causes the body to restore cells back to normal homeostasis — by regenerating tissue, healing wounds and knitting bone together. No drug in the world can do that, but that seems to be all that physicians know about — drugs. And if that's all they know, how can they promote something they *don't know*? How can they promote health and recommend cures, when *they do not even know what the terms mean?*

I think about my own experience with doctors. I remember going to a dermatologist as a teenager with acne problems. I asked him if diet had anything to do with my problem. He just mumbled something and handed me a prescription for tetracycline. That was some years ago, but they are still doing the same thing today. I suffered from debilitating menstrual cramps that one time sent me to urgent care. I was given Darvon that made me vomit. I have made many trips to the doctor throughout my life for a variety of ailments and never once did *any* doctor or nurse or any other health professional ask me *what I ate*. No physician ever addressed why I had acne or why I had cramps. Each time I went to a physician, all they ever wanted to do for me was prescribe drugs, drugs, drugs, and more drugs.

Only thirty percent of medical schools in America offer courses in nutrition; and of the ones that do, only thirty percent require them. The courses that are taught are brief and mainly concerned with which foods are contraindicated for certain drugs. In other words, they are essentially worthless. I remember asking a friend of mine who was a third-year medical student about nutrition classes. He said he'd never taken one and didn't plan on taking any, either. Why? Because it wasn't required. Medical school is grueling. The average med student isn't going to take a course he doesn't have to. He's just trying to get though.

Unfortunately, physicians are not interested in preventing disease. They are concerned only with treating it, not figuring out why you got it. They are concerned with crisis care, not prevention. They put out fires, so to speak, and the main way they do this is through drugs and surgery. Let me be clear here, this author is not disparaging the crisis care system in the U.S. If you have been mangled in a car accident you want to go to someone who can put you back together; you lose a finger, you want to go to someone who can sew it back on; you have a stroke or a heart attack; you want someone who can pull you through it. That "someone" would be a medical doctor. But you do *not* want to go to an MD if you want to rid yourself of a chronic condition, or if you want to know how to keep from getting one. Because the truth is, your physician has no idea how you got it, how to cure it, or how to keep you from getting it again. There are a number of reasons for this. Medical doctors are usually very busy and have little time for research and reading, especially if they are part of an HMO. They are also subject to the AMA's big-brotheresque behavior, and certainly don't want the hassle of a possible investigation if they try something outside of what they've been taught. And then there is the arrogance factor. Doctors who have spent their lives acquiring knowledge that is far beyond that of a layperson are not likely to listen to someone who does not possess this knowledge — especially if the person suggests that solutions to health problems could be found through a change of diet and lifestyle. Doing so would require that they re-evaluate their entire medical education and could even mean contemplating the possibility that most of what they learned in medical school about health was *wrong*. That would be quite a pill to swallow. But there is another reason and probably the strongest of all — economics. It would not be economically feasible for the *disease industry*.

Please understand, *we do not have a health system in this nation. What we have is a disease industry.* The AMA promotes a disease industry, and that's big business. The cancer industry is no exception; in fact, it's a billion dollar business. There are more people in it than simply those who have the disease. There are doctors, nurses, radiologists, the insurance companies, pharmaceutical companies, prosthesis manufacturers, the morticians and the list goes on. There is no money to be made from telling people *how* to keep from getting sick. There is no money in anything that keeps a person from going to the doctor to receive extensive tests with complex diagnostics. Think about it. What if our citizens really were to truly adopt a healthful way of living? What then? What if we had no physicians to prescribe drugs? No radiologists to administer radiation? No pharmaceutical companies to manufacture drugs like chemo, insulin, high blood pressure medicine, high cholesterol medicine, heart disease medicine, etc.? No pharmacists to fill them? No insurance company for you to pay? What then? The medical machine would shut down overnight. Then what would happen? What would all these people do? I know of a woman who is a sales representative for a pharmaceutical company. She has a beautiful home in an exclusive part of town. She refers to it as "The House that Cancer Built." She's not exaggerating.

I've had clients who've corrected their own conditions where the doctors had no answers. When they related their success to their physicians — instead of being elated and wanting to know how they did it — they were either berated or silenced. Why? *Why would a doctor not be interested in something that could help someone?*

Perhaps the physicians themselves are afraid. Historically, the AMA and medical community have had no mercy on anyone who goes against what's considered orthodox. Consider the fact that physicians in California can be stripped of their medical license if they prescribe for cancer anything other than poisoning, burning, or cutting (i.e. chemotherapy, radiation or surgery). Consider the plight of Harry Hoxley. In the 1920s he developed an effective herbal, non-toxic remedy for cancer. When he refused to sell it to Morris Fishbein (the president of the AMA) because Fishbein would not agree to give it to poor people, Hoxley was hounded from one end of this country to the other. Eventually he had to close his clinics. The medical genius Max Gerson was treated the same way when he advocated dietary remedies for most physical problems. His clinic ended up in Mexico. And so it continues today. Any one who bucks the system pays a severe price. This is not to suggest that all FDA and AMA employees, doctors, nurses, radiologists and others in the field are in some vast conspiracy to keep people sick and on drugs, although sometimes you might think so. These people and their families get cancer and other life threatening illnesses just like anyone else. But they are deceived in that they truly believe what they have been taught — drugs and medical intervention are the *only* ways to health. Yes, medical interventions have saved millions of lives. No one could dispute that. However, not every health challenge can or should be thought of in terms of pathogenic forces that need to be controlled. Hormonal issues come to mind as cutting-edge scientists are now realizing that balance in this area is a matter of biophysics.

Isn't it interesting that there have been times in the history of medicine when what was considered orthodox and necessary is later considered barbaric? Bloodletting, the withdrawal of considerable amounts of blood by cutting into a vein (by knife or lancet) is an example. It was even prescribed for infants, and those already weak and ill. In fact, bloodletting was so respected that a major British medical journal called itself *Lancet,* and still uses that name today.[2] Benjamin Rush (1745-1813) a signatory of the Declaration of Independence and considered the father of modern medicine, declared that any physician not bloodletting their patients should be considered a "quack." George Washington was treated with this "therapy" following a horseback riding accident Almost 1.7 liters of blood was withdrawn, contributing to his death by a throat infection in 1799.[3] Bloodletting has been abandoned for all but a few conditions and even then, it is rarely used.

This is just one of the many examples where the respected medical authorities of the day were wrong, often dead wrong. Perhaps in the near future chemotherapy, radiation and open-heart surgery will also be considered barbaric and dangerous, validating the dissenters today who are also considered "quacks."

This author believes that there is a war raging against the use of natural means to cure and prevent disease. It is being fought at the highest levels of the health and political arenas and it will not let up until those involved either control the alternative

---

[2] Dana Ullman, Discovering Homeopathy: Medicine for the 21st Century, 1988
[3] ibid

medicine field. If Codex Alimentarius has its way in the US, all supplements including vitamins, minerals, herbs, nutraceuticals will be regulated.[4] Vitamin B6 (pyridoxamine), a natural occurring substance, has officially been classified by the FDA as a drug. Now any nutritional supplements containing pyridoxamine can be considered **adulterated and illegal** by the FDA, which may raid vitamin companies and seize products.

In July of 2009, The National Institute of Health [NIH] released a study stating that Americans in 2007 spent a whopping 33.9 **billion out-of-pocket dollars** on alternative health care.[5] According to statistics, $22.0 billion was spent on self-care costs— informational classes and products, such as fish oil, herbs and nutraceuticals ($14.8 billion). What's interesting is this figure **does not** include products such as vitamins and minerals, **which would only increase the number!** U.S. adults also spent approximately $11.9 billion on an estimated 354.2 million visits to alternative medicine practitioners such as acupuncturists, natural health consultants, chiropractors, massage therapists, etc. To put these figures in context, the $14.8 billion spent on natural products is equivalent to approximately one-third of total out-of-pocket spending on prescription drugs, and the $11.9 billion spent on alternative health practitioner visits is equivalent to approximately one-quarter of total out-of-pocket spending on physician visits. While this is very good news for

---

[4] Codex Alimentarius established by the UN in 1962, sets advisory standards concerning free-trade foods. See www.healthfreedomusa.org
[5] http://nccam.nih.gov/news/camstats/costs/

21

anyone contemplating entering the field of natural health, understand that Big Pharma is certainly trying to get a piece of the pie. There are groups trying to make supplements that have been widely available for decades, available only to licensed health practitioners. But this has not happened yet, so press on. These numbers show that Americans are figuring it out!

Ok. I've made my point. You get it. America needs all natural health practitioners it can get. It needs you. Your goal is nothing short of changing the health-paradigm of the entire nation — one person at a time. Yes, you are going to have your critics and naysayers, but just remember, if those in the medical establishment were doing their jobs, there would be no need for people like you. No, it's not going to be easy and you shouldn't wish it to be. As the old saying goes, wish that your efforts be worth it. And when your first client thanks you profoundly with tears in his eyes for giving him his life back, it will be. So let's get on with it and get you equipped to start your own natural health consulting business!

Credentials

You should go to school and obtain credentials if you want to become a professional practitioner. Other than the fact that you need to be educated on the basics in your field, mainstream America is accustomed to health practitioners with letters after their names. People will be reluctant to seek your services unless you have them, even if you have been studying on your own for 20+ years and are superbly self-taught. After all, it's what MDs and other medical practitioners do. They go to schools and they study.

Another reason you need credentials, and a big one: most clients want to see results as quickly as possible. To do that they need supplements. The majority of supplement companies — the good ones anyway — require a practitioner to furnish proof that they are credentialed to distribute them and (many say they sell only to *licensed* professionals, but they mean *credentialed*) and acceptance is up to the discretion of the company. Normally accepted are: Certified Nutritionist (CN), Certified Clinical Nutritionist (CCN), Certified Nutritional Consultant (CNC), Chiropractor (DC), Naturopath (ND), Licensed Acupuncturist, (L. Ac), Homeopath (DHom), and Osteopath (DO), to name a few. And of course, there are Medical Doctors, (MDs), Nurses (NPs and RNs), Registered Dieticians (RDs), and Physical Therapists (PTs), although these practitioners rarely use them. Most companies will accept certificates from an iridologist, herbologist, and a colon hydrotherapist as well. They will also usually accept a BS, MS and a PhD nutritional degree. But a certificate as a massage therapist will not usually qualify, nor will that of a personal trainer, reflexologist, yoga or Pilates instructor. Again, it's up to the company. I do know of professionals in the fitness field who do nutritional counseling and send their clients to health stores for their supplements. My opinion is that there are very few over-the-counter brands that are actually decent, let alone therapeutic, even in health food stores. And people these days are so toxic and nutritionally deficient, they definitely need potent supplements to obtain results.

Network marketing companies will take anyone. Building a business with network marketing products using natural health consulting as your venue is a subject we will discuss in more detail later on.

Being credentialed will do something else for you — and this is huge. The vast majority of what I know about natural health I did *not* learn in school. I learned it from attending lectures, seminars and webinars sponsored by supplement companies. True, these seminars are designed to educate practitioners on their product lines, but the peripheral information you'll receive will be invaluable. I go to every seminar I can and these have helped me immensely. I have also learned a great deal through local workshops I've attended with fellow practitioners. Again, I had to have the necessary letters next to my name before I could gain entrance to any of them.

All right, let's recap. The four main reasons for getting credentials as a natural health consultant are: (1) you need to learn basic natural health principles. (2) People like to see letters after your name if they are going to entrust you with something valuable, especially their health. They think it means you know something. Let's hope it does, but we're talking perception, here. Mainstream is what we're going after and it equates letters with knowledge. (3) To have an effective practice, you need effective supplements. People want to see results as quickly as possible. That almost always requires supplemental help, either herbal, nutraceutical, concentrated food or homeopathic. The good companies require credentials to get their products. (4) Credentials open the door for you to learn further by attending seminars designed for practitioners.

So we've established that you do need credentials. The next questions are what kind and from where? In what direction should you go? That depends on what you want to do. This book is designed for people who want to consult with clients and be paid. If that is you, please know that although natural health is an upcoming field in the United States, there is no real clear path to follow. As the FDA and AMA have yet to devise a way to regulate this emerging breed of practitioners (believe me, they're trying), there is no definitive direction required by law. This is both good news and not so good news. Good, because you are free to pick and choose the path you want to follow, not so good because the field of natural health abounds with nuts, flakes, charlatans, snake-oil salesmen, misinformation and just plain lies. And there's a bunch of schools out there whose diplomas aren't worth the paper they're printed on.

I advise picking a school and program that's within your budget, meets your schedule, has the best curriculum, and will teach you what you want to know. And it must agree with your viewpoint. I would never, for example become an RD even though most of mainstream America knows what a Registered Dietician is. Why? Besides the fact that they're taught government-sanctioned health information that is for the most part, useless, these are the people who do hospital menus. I'll never forget when a man I knew ended up in the hospital with a heart attack. The first meal they gave him after surgery was pork chops, mashed potatoes with margarine and cola. Need I say more?

Below is a list and descriptions of some options to explore to help you in your decision, along with some commentary. It is by no means exhaustive, but will show some paths commonly taken. If you find one that appeals to you: *do your homework.* Find people who have gone to the schools, earned the degree, or become certified, and talk to them. Most are happy to give their honest opinions concerning their experience. Some schools and programs sound much better on paper than they really are and some are better than they sound on paper, so take some time and make the right decision.

Options

CCN is a Certified Clinical Nutritionist. Eligibility requirements to be certified as a CCN are as follows: a minimum Bachelors Degree in science; minimum of 19 science-course credits, 14 human-nutrition-course credits along with 900 hours of clinical nutrition. Candidates must also complete an internship, as well as a postgraduate course designed specifically for clinical nutrition. They must also complete an exam by the International and American Association of Clinical Nutrition (I.A.A.C.N) and 20 hours of continuing education annually. Obviously, this is a very involved course of study; however, the designation is highly respected and graduates are well trained.

CNC stands for Certified Nutritional Consultant. The certification program is administered by the Commission on Certification of the American Association of Nutritional Consultants (A.A.N.C.). Candidates are required to complete a series of exams designed to demonstrate proficiency in the areas of nutrition and practice management.

CN is a Certified Nutritionist. This designation is usually given to those who have completed a college-level, two-year, six-course program that includes a proctored examination. Course work includes public health and wellness awareness, anatomy and physiology, general nutrition, clinical nutrition, alternative therapies, practice management and case studies.

Offered by the American Health Science University, the program is also offered as a distance learning option. After completion of the program, all graduates are required to apply for and maintain the private CN license each year. Also, continuing education requirements must be also be met annually. A CN license is a private license and is differentiated from a state license.

A Registered Dietician (RD) training system involves attendance at an American Dietetics Association (ADA) approved, undergraduate dietetics program. The student is required to complete a supervised 900-hour internship approved by the ADA, under the direction of an RD. Upon completion of the internship, the student is eligible to take the ADA Registered Dietician examination. Successful completion leads to the RD credential. The average dietician program heavily emphasizes conventional dietary philosophy and intervention, as well as mass food management, distribution, and safety. The RD in the past has rarely used nutritional supplementation and has been traditionally resistant, even hostile, to the idea.

Degrees from Distance Learning/Online Schools Specializing in Natural Health /Nutrition can give bachelors, masters, doctorates of philosophy (PhDs) and naturopathy (we'll discuss naturopathy and naturopaths in some detail) degrees. This is a very attractive option for many people. Most of them offer a wide variety of pertinent courses and viewpoints on the relevant subjects. They are also usually affordable and normally offer flexible payment plans. And given the fact they are distance learning, you will determine the pace at which you'll proceed with your courses. Now that's good if you're motivated, not good if you let everything in your life take precedent over your studies; an easy thing to do. This educational option will require you exercise discipline and effective time-management.

A degree in traditional naturopathy usually requires a bachelor's degree, but not always. If you don't already have one, many schools have programs where you can start at the beginning. How long it will take depends on you. But even if it takes you four or five years, so what? Time is going to pass whether you participate or not, so why not do it? Then when you earn a bachelor's degree, you'll be eligible to start your business and attend supplement company- sponsored lectures.

Which school should you enroll in? There are, of course, questions you should ask to help you make your decision. Here are some of them: (1) are the courses and textbooks relevant and up to date? As new information is being discovered all the time, you want to be sure that your school is cutting-edge. (2) Will the textbooks be good resources for future use? Remember, you are going to have to buy these books. (3) How about the faculty, are they qualified to design the programs and grade your papers? Have they been in the natural health field for a while? My personal feeling is that someone with a bachelor's degree should not be grading a master's candidate's work, but it happens. And here's a touchy subject with me; I don't think medical doctors should be teaching courses at a natural health school unless they themselves have been trained and educated in natural health with advanced degrees or credentials. Some natural health schools employ MDs because they feel it gives them credibility with the public The reasoning is understandable, but medical doctors still need to be trained just like anyone else. Otherwise, they're not qualified. (4) Does the school have a good system to help you to get to where you want to go? The school I attended provided a step-by-step guide on how to write a publishable PhD dissertation, outlining exactly what I needed to do. I can't tell you how valuable it was when I was writing mine. (5) Are they in good financial standing? You don't want to sign on with a school then have them go out of business soon after.

Beware of schools that offer degrees based on "life experience." Some are legitimate, but you should check them out. When I see that I think: diploma mill. Credibility and professionalism are key in our field, and since we don't yet have the acceptance orthodox medicine does, we must strive for the highest standards we can.

Those are just a few things to inquire about when selecting a distance/online school and I'm sure you can come up with many more. Write down your questions and get them answered *to your satisfaction.*

What may be a negative for some is: that almost all of the natural health schools are privately accredited, meaning they are not accredited in the traditional sense. Accreditation is a complex and controversial issue. This can be a subject of concern for non-licensed practitioners and gets into the whole discussion, is a degree from one of these schools a "real degree." To answer that question one might ask, what is a "real school?" Is there "real" learning going on? Are the instructors qualified to teach what they are teaching? Are the textbooks and reading material sufficient to teach the intended subject matter? Are the students required to demonstrate evidence that they have sufficiently mastered an area of study? If so, then the answer is yes, the school in question is "real." But, there are drawbacks to obtaining a degree from one. No traditionally accredited institution or government agency will recognize a degree from a privately accredited school. This means you cannot transfer credits from a privately accredited institution to one that is traditionally accredited, nor could you teach there. Now with that having been said, there are those that have broken the barrier in that regard. But at this writing, that is highly unusual. There are also some states that in order to practice nutrition, you must have a degree from a USDE-accredited school, or work under a licensed health practitioner. We'll discuss the various terms and issues concerning accreditation in detail in the next chapter.

Some pronounced pluses concerning privately accredited natural health schools are these: first, they are normally *much* less expensive than USDE-accredited schools. And some of them include the books and study guides with the tuition. Next, you will get a totally focused education on natural health. You will not have to take English, history or courses like that. At this writing there is at least one online school in the US offering a USDE accredited bachelor's degree in alternative medicine. But the education is not nearly as focused on natural health as what you'll get from a privately accredited school, as you must take a number of courses not relevant to field. But that's what's required by the USDE if you want the traditional accreditation.

An important fact you must be aware of and not a pleasant one: there is legislation in some states attempting to make criminals out of anyone who advertises themselves with credentials from a non-USDE accredited school. Texas has this on the books, as does Oregon. That means if you live in either of these states and you try to obtain clientele and/or using a degree or certificate from a privately accredited natural health school, you could be charged with a misdemeanor. Now whether it would hold up in a court of law is another matter. In 2004 three graduates from a privately accredited school licensed in Wyoming challenged the Oregon law and won. The judge did stipulate however, that graduates must disclose to prospective employers and clients that their degree is non-government accredited. As I said, the fight is real. Enrollment in non-traditional online/distance schools is increasing while in traditional schools, it's declining. Maybe that's part of the reason for this horrendous legislation. That and the fact that the education natural health schools provide pose a serious threat to Big Pharma, and the medical profession in general. At this writing Texas and Oregon are the only states with this nonsense in place. But who knows what the future will hold. Be aware of this law and how it could pertain to your state.

Another salient point concerning privately accredited, online/distance natural health schools; none of them qualify you to become licensed in anything. The legalities of licensing will be discussed in an upcoming section, but you must always remember this because you do not want to overstep your legal bounds — something practitioners do all the time. A list of schools is in the appendix. If you find one you are interested in, do your due diligence.

Many new to the field are becoming **naturopaths.** Naturopathy is a broad area of study, the term being coined in the US around 1900 by John Scheel and used by Benedict Lust. It is defined as a system of non-invasive and drugless health-care dealing with root causes. Its main concern is getting to the core of health challenges by determining why problems may exist. Naturopathy focuses on prevention. Believing that sickness, pain and physical degeneration are the consequence of breaking biochemical laws, it advocates adhering to these laws, thereby preventing illness and undesirable physical conditions. There are two kinds of naturopaths, licensed and unlicensed. Let's look at the difference between the two.

Traditional naturopaths do not heal, treat, diagnose or cure any disease. They use education and counseling and recommend the most natural substances possible, such as a toxin-free diet, whole-food, natural vitamins, herbs, homeopathy, exercise, clean water, rest, etc. They may or may not have assessment devices in their offices but if so, they are always non-invasive. They are usually regarded as alternative or complementary practitioners rather than primary care providers. Training programs for traditional naturopaths vary greatly, but none provide the allopathic education and clinical experience of the naturopathic medical schools.

Traditional naturopaths are best described as natural health educators. They cannot draw blood, use intervenous devices (such as vitamin C drips), prescibe drugs, inject needles or do anything else that requires a license. There are online schools offering programs in traditional naturopathy, but at this writing none in the US hold any USDE accreditation.

Naturopathic physicians (ND) are licensed naturopaths. Presently, there are only seven schools in North America that offer programs to qualify for licensing: Bastyr University; Washington, National College of Natural Medicine; Illinois, National University of Health Sciences; Illinois, College of Naturopathic Medicine; Connecticut, Southwest College of Naturopathic Medicine; Arizona, Canadian College of Naturopathic Medicine; Ontario and Boucher Institute of Naturopathic Medicine in British Columbia. At this writing, at least 15 states in the US plus the District of Columbia license naturopaths: Alaska, Arizona, California, Connecticut, Hawaii, Idaho, Kansas, Maine, Minnesota, Montana, New Hampshire, Oregon, Utah, Vermont and Washington. Others are considering

34

licensing. In addition, Guam, Puerto Rico and the U.S. Virgin Islands also have licensing laws.

Naturopathic physicians can be viewed as primary care providers and are trained in conventional medical science, diagnosis and treatments, although not fully. They can perform physical examinations, gynecological exams, nutritional and dietary assessments. They may also order laboratory testing, metabolic analysis, allergy testing, X-ray examinations, and other diagnostic tests. Furthermore, they can prescribe certain drugs such as antibiotics and bio-identical hormones. In addition to training in western medical approaches, they are (of course) trained in nutrition, botanical medicine, homeopathy, and other natural therapeutics.

Although this might seem an attractive career path, there are some issues that must be considered. First, although NDs are considered physicians, very few insurance companies recognize them as such. That means their practices will be cash only unless they partner with an MD — something most MDs are reluctant to do because of the malpractice issue. Secondly, the schools that license NDs are medical schools. That means that unless you are independently wealthy, you will finish in four or five years (longer if you work while attending) owing a lot of money. Thus, your office fees will need to be high to recoup your costs. That does *not* mean however, that you couldn't build a large practice, because you certainly could. However, it *does* mean that you would need to be very good at marketing (we'll discuss how to do that later) because you would not have the referral base MDs receive from insurance companies.

One more point I will make about becoming a licensed ND. Consider this fact; an ND has all restrictions of being medical doctor, yet *none* of the benefits. Technically they're physicians, yet they cannot work in hospitals, can't even practice what they've leaned in certain states (chiropractic and acupuncture). And as previously mentioned, rarely can they collect insurance. In the world of orthodox medicine, they're second-class doctors. They're glorified Physician Assistants and Nurse Practitioners in the sense that if they write scripts, they have to do so under a licensed MD. I am not saying things will never change. From what I understand, Kaiser Permanente, CA is going to be hiring NDs for its HMOs (I also hear that they're going to be paid a lot less than MDs). But, that is certainly not the case in most states. In fact, some states, such as South Carolina and Tennessee, outlaw naturopathic licensing altogether. So, it's going to be an uphill battle for sometime. If I wanted to become a licensed physician and practice integrative medicine, I'd go to one of the medical schools in the Caribbean as they are much less expensive than those in the US (you'd be eligible for licensing in America). Then I'd take additional studies through one of the online, natural health schools. I think that would be a much better option than becoming a licensed naturopathic physician.

You must also consider the mindset of the average American: you have two doctors, one accepts insurance, and one doesn't. Which one would a person most likely go to? The MD because to that person a doctor is a doctor. Now on the other hand, when he comes to you, he'll expect to pay cash *because he knows the difference between a consultant and a physician* (if you've done your job, that is). It's all a matter of perception. *People expect primary care physicians to take insurance.*

It's not easy for licensed naturopaths. In my opinion, they're in no-man's land. They're not fully alternative practitioners, yet they're not thoroughly trained medical doctors either. And to some people that means that means they're not "real" doctors. Although it is probably the highest regarded credential in the field of natural health, there are definite challenges that accompany it. Think long and hard as to whether you're are up to those challenges.

If you are a chiropractor and you want to incorporate nutritional counseling into your practice, good for you! You have great credentials. The public already thinks of you as an alternative health practitioner, but you still need to learn as your chiropractic school taught you very little in the way of nutrition. Go to as many seminars on nutrition as you can. You may want to go to a distance school as some offer programs tailored specifically to professionals already in the health field.

Naturopathy for animals will probably be the next big wave in natural health care. At this writing there is only one natural health school offering a full-on comprehensive degree program in alternative health care for animals, and that is the *Kingdom College of Natural Health*. I think this a field showing great promise. It is wide open and the information and expertise is desperately needed and desired. Most people will do almost anything for their pets, and they too are suffering diseases resulting from a toxic diet and deficiencies. Many of their owners are realizing that natural is the way to go for long-term health. But be aware, the traditional veterinary field right now is extremely hostile to natural animal care. Most vets are even further behind the curve on this issue than traditional MDs. And that's saying a lot! But if you have a leaning towards animal-care, you may want to consider becoming a doctor of animal naturopathy.

There are also certificates with titles you can get through course programs from distance schools such as holistic health practitioner, natural health consultant, natural health educator, etc. Upon completion, you will receive a certificate with your name and title. You may also earn certificates in herbology, iridology, sclerology and more. You should be able to set up a natural health consulting business with any of them, it just depends on what you want and can do with your time, money and effort.

Now with all the above being said, here's the truth of the matter. The majority of your clients will not even ask where your credentials are from. Yes, they will want you to have *some* from *somewhere*, but as long as you help them, *they will not care.* Generally, the only people who ask me where I went to school are other practitioners. The bottom line is this: you help them, they will come. As in any field, the cream rises to the top.

Accreditation

I'll never forget this incident. I was working a booth at a natural health fair in Los Angeles promoting a product. I was discussing health with a woman who was a registered nurse. She asked me where I went to school, trying to determine whether I was "qualified" to talk about the subject at hand. I told her its name and she said, "Oh, that's not a *real* school. What do you mean," I asked. She smugly answered, "It's not accredited." I will tell you what my response was to that ignorant and arrogant comment at the end of this section and I hope that if the "real school" issue is a problem for you, we can put it to rest.

In the United States, there is an abundance of terms regarding accreditation (or other similar statuses) used by groups, educational institutions, accrediting commissions, and states. Here are some definitions that should help you if you're confused about the various terms appearing in catalogs and advertisements.

Accreditation: A term used frequently used by educational institutions. Although some institutions use the term *accredited*, it is of little value and does not guarantee any legal rights or good standing within any of the 50 states. There are various accrediting agencies that are not recognized by the U.S. Department of Education.

Regional Accreditation: Four of these accrediting commissions (i.e., agencies) exist in the United States covering the North, South, East, and Western regions of the country. They are considered the standard commissions/agencies of governmental accreditation and are legally permitted to accredit institutions that meet certain criteria. Originally established by the U.S. Government after World War II to help veterans acquire scholarships and education, regional accrediting commissions accredit nearly all state universities, colleges, and other various institutes of learning. Once an educational institution acquires regional accreditation, monies may be obtained for grants, scholarships, etc. In some cases, money may be obtained from the U.S. Government to operate and pay for the daily expenses of the educational institution. This is the type of accreditation meant when the average person asks, "Is a school accredited?"

National Accreditation: This is recognized by the U.S. Department of Education and mainly applies to vocational schools. However, in most circles, *National Accreditation* is not as well respected as *Regional Accreditation.* Holding National Accreditation does not guarantee college scholarship monies from the U.S. Government.

Distance Education and Training Council (DETC): is an accrediting agency recognized by the United States Department of Education. Founded in 1926, its scope is accrediting distance/correspondence/online schools. Although USDE recognized, DETC accreditation is the least respected of the government accrediting commissions. At this writing, some regionally and nationally accredited schools will not accept degrees or courses from schools with this accreditation. This will most likely change, however. Online learning with downloadable CDs, DVDs, webinars and blogs is already establishing itself as a viable and desirable way of learning.

Private Accreditation: At the present time, nearly all natural health colleges and institutes hold some kind of private accreditation, because the public demands it. Private accreditation does give some degree of confidence to the public, although it is relatively easy to obtain. Be informed that no state or governmental accrediting agency or state university will recognize any privately owned accrediting commission, organization, or society, regardless of any claims to the contrary.

Affiliated: This term generally means an institution/school is connected in some manner to another educational institution (i.e., university, college, association, organization, or group). However, in a strict sense, the term *affiliate* is technically a division of some other entity usually considered the parent organization. With this in mind, it is important to know that certain universities and colleges allow educational institutions/schools to affiliate under certain conditions and criteria established by officials of the parent institution. In some instances, the subordinate school may be charged a one-time fee or ongoing fee to be considered "in good standing" with the parent organization. The power of a school that is "affiliated" with another educational institution may be limited, or in some cases there may be no limitations placed on the affiliated school (i.e., subordinate institution) whatsoever. In a legal sense, the parent organization may be responsible for the claims and actions of an affiliated institution.

Approved or Exempt: Some states permit the use of these terms for non-traditional colleges, but neither *approved* nor *exempt* means an educational institution is licensed by the state. Approved or exempt are terms that mean an institution has been granted permission to operate within the boundaries of a state if certain criteria are met.

Authorized: The State of California allows the term *authorized college* or sometimes *state authorized* for some non-traditional educational institutions. This does not mean such an institution is *state licensed*, nor does it mean it is recognized by the U.S. Department of Education. Most state departments of higher education monitor such colleges that hold this status, closely.

Certificate: Any association, organization, or educational institution may legally grant a certificate in almost any field or for any amount of study in most states. Usually certificates require a period of study from three to six months. However, some institutions may require a longer period of study depending on their criteria. NOTE: A certificate is not a diploma, academic instrument, or degree.

Certified: The term *certified* causes the public to take notice and assume that a respected group/agency is attesting to the skill of an individual in a particular field. For example, there are certified mechanics, body shops, plumbers, accountants, electricians, small-engine repair shops, etc. Groups often gain a voice within states merely because a large number of people have joined their ranks and desire to possess the title *certified*. The bottom line is, the term certified is no better than the group, association, organization, or agency that grants it. Not all organizations that grant certification to individuals are reliable, respected, accountable, or honest.

Degree: A *degree* is regulated by most states up to a point. In the field of education, a degree is considered an academic legal instrument granted by a college or university to a student who has completed a prescribed course of study. A non-accredited distance learning institution is usually given the status of "approved." However, this does not mean a college is licensed or accredited by the state where the institution is domiciled.

Designation: The term *designation* does not mean *degree*. A small number of natural health colleges in the United States, not legally permitted to offer a degree in certain states, now use the term designation for a certain study (i.e., some offer a designation in naturopathy). Webster's dictionary gives the meaning of designation as: "the act of pointing out; a specific indication; or that which designates; a distinguishing name, title, etc." Certain colleges using the term, *designation* are rapidly gaining acceptance in America. Students falsely believe they have earned a *degree* when they are the holder of a *designation,* which is *not* an academic instrument.

Diploma: Any association, organization, or educational institution may legally grant a "diploma" for the completion or study of some subject or field. Diplomas may be obtained within one to three years of supervised educational study. A diploma is not a degree, and is not considered an academic instrument in most states. However, there are exceptions. Some states require the same criteria for a diploma as for a degree. When one wants to obtain a diploma from an educational institution, it is best to contact the post-secondary educational division (sometimes known as the Proprietary Educational Division) of the state where the institution is domiciled to determine the legal status of a diploma.

Diploma Mill: Usually an unregulated higher education with substandard academic requirements or none at all. There are individuals and organizations who profess that *any* organization not USDE accredited is a diploma mill. This is incorrect. There are many quality schools *not* recognized by the US Department of Education, as many do not want to be regulated. Numerous natural health schools fall this category, but they are not diploma mills as they do offer quality education. Most people do not realize that before a school can be USDE accredited, it must be in operation for at least two years. Accreditation is a long process and can take many years. So, during the time the school is pursuing accreditation and is operating, is it a diploma mill? And then when it receives accreditation, is it all the sudden legitimate? USDE accreditation is not the standard as to whether a school is a diploma mill or not. It's not even a standard as to whether a school is good or not. Accreditation guarantees that a school has met certain standards and that is all.

Registered: Some colleges of natural health are only required to "register" in a state if they qualify under a religious not-for-profit 501(c) 3 exception status granted by the Internal Revenue Service. States take no responsibility for the claims or actions of such colleges. However, states have had to fix problems created by such institutions if they lack ethical practices, substandard education or have no self-imposed accountability. At the present time, there is a crackdown in all 50 states and U.S. territories on natural health colleges operating under the 501(c) 3 not-for-profit tax-exempt status. However, religious institutions are permitted to award religious degrees in certain fields, although they may not be "accredited."

Some natural health commissions also offer various certificates granting individuals titles such as: registered naturopath, registered homeopath, or registered natural health practitioner, and sometimes the "practitioner" may be referred to as "consultant." The term *registered* gives the practitioner no legal authority in the 50 states and U.S. territories, but will capture the attention of the public when one holds such a certificate. The idea of the term *registered* is for the holder to appear legitimate.

State Licensed: To obtain a state license is difficult, to say the least. Some states follow the same criteria as that established by regional accrediting commissions and some don't. Although the term *state licensed* is not completely understood by the public, a degree that is *state licensed* is seen by some as having more value and significance than a degree accredited by a private accrediting agency. It is not to be confused however, as the same type of licensing for chiropractors, physicians, etc.

State Registered: This term carries no legal standing. It simply means the educational institution is permitted to operate in the state without accreditation, license, or approval from the state.

So, what does this all mean? I can only tell you what it means to me — not a whole lot. And that leads me to share the response I gave the woman who inferred I was not qualified to speak about health because I didn't go to a "real" (USDE accredited) school. She had told me she was a nurse. So, with that, I asked her, "Do you know the meaning of the phrase "iatrogenic death?" Silence was her response. I continued with, "It means death induced by medical procedures, usually by drug reactions, surgeries and/or diagnostic procedures, *even when administered correctly.*" Again, she did not respond. I then asked, "Are you aware of how many people die each year from iatrogenesis? Thousands. In fact by many reports, it's the third leading cause of death in America. So why would I want to learn health from institutions that train those responsible for such deaths?"

Why, indeed. A traditional, regionally accredited university was not going to teach what I needed and wanted to know. I could have attended one and earned a degree in nutrition, but decided my time and money could be better spent. I chose a non-traditional, privately accredited school that had what I needed; not hospital nutrition or a lot of useless jargon with theories. My choice was a good one and has suited my clients and me quite well. So no, my degree is not recognized by government agencies or government-accredited schools. Yes, I do on occasion, run into the typical American drones who think that because my degree and education is not recognized by the USDE, the medical community or some other "authority figure," it's not valid. *I don't care.* I have helped many people and isn't that the point? I once had a client who had suffered for 15 years from colitis. He'd been to countless medical doctors with no success. He even had surgery, but with no success. I taught him how to eat correctly and recommended the supplements that would support him holistically. Within two weeks, he was "feeling 90% better and had his life back" (his words, not mine). Do you think he for one minute, *cares* who accredited the school I attended? Your clients won't care either.

Perhaps government-sponsored accrediting agencies will wake up and notice that the public is leaving the medical establishment in large numbers and is looking to those educated in non-traditional schools for solutions. Maybe then they will start accrediting some of these natural health schools, I don't know. But for now, it is what it is. Just find the school that teaches you what you need to know in order to help people return to the principles of true health.

Legal Issues

As a natural health practitioner, you must be very clear as to what your legal parameters are. In the past, there are those who were not and paid the price. Businesses were shut down, files and equipment were confiscated and some even faced jail time. You have a right to practice as a nutritional consultant, but you must avoid at all costs practicing medicine without a license. What does that mean? It means not representing yourself as a licensed practitioner and not doing what it is they do.

In most states, the definition of practicing medicine is similar. I suggest that you go online or write to your State Medical Board and find out exactly what your state says, but basically it's going to say something like this: A person shall be regarded as practicing medicine of he uses the words or letters, MD, DSC, Pod. D, ND (check your state) or any other title that implies he is connected with the practice of surgery, podiatry, medicine or midwifery. If he/she examines and diagnoses for compensation, and then prescribes, advises, or recommends a treatment, and/or then dispenses for compensation directly or indirectly, a drug, medicine, mold, cast, appliance, prescribes or administers X-rays, performs an operation for the relief or cure of a wound, fracture, bodily injury, infirmity or disease, he/she is practicing medicine (unless the treatment is through prayer alone).[6] You are also in violation if you draw blood or recommend your client discontinue physician-prescribed medication.

What you say and don't say is key. Your language is what will either keep you in practice or get you in trouble, so always be aware what you say and how you say it. I was at a social gathering and was asked by a woman what I do for a living. When I responded she then asked, "What do you do for arthritis?" I responded, "I do nothing for arthritis, but rather I help people with arthritis to attain optimal health." What did I say? Nothing and everything, totally within my legal boundaries. The typical, uninformed natural health consultant when asked that same question would have most likely spouted off a number of supplements as being good for arthritis. If the consultant had collected money from the woman for that information, he/she would have technically been guilty of practicing medicine without a license. Why? Because arthritis is classified as a medical, diagnosable disease and by naming supplements specifically for the condition, the consultant was setting a therapeutic course, *which is against the law*. It happens all the time. Some researchers estimate that up to 80% of natural health consultants are guilty of practicing medicine without a license, regardless of what system they use.

Here's how you'd handle this. You would say, "If it were me and I had arthritis, I would take the following

---

[6] Practicing Medicine Without a License, Chester Yozwick, 1985

supplements and eat the following foods." You would not say, "Take these supplements for arthritis and eat this diet." If you did, again, technically you would be naming a disease with a cure. *Natural or not, you'd still be recommending a cure which is against the law.* Here's another scenario: someone comes to you with diabetes. Are you going to say, "Take XYZ as it will reduce your blood sugar, strengthen your pancreas, and over time with a good diet, cure your diabetes?" You do and that client happens to be an incognito representative from your State Medical Board, you could be busted. You've used the word "diabetes" and "cure" along with your recommended protocol. But if you say, "If it were me and I had diabetes, I would take XYZ as it could help reduce my blood sugar and strengthen my pancreas," you'll be fine and within the law. That falls under the category of dispensing information, which is perfectly legal. You could also say," studies have shown people with diabetes taking XYZ have shown improvement." That's also acceptable as again, you are just dispensing information. Now you may be thinking, well, that's merely semantics. True, but these are semantics that will keep you in business and out of trouble. Get into the habit of using yourself as an example when talking about diseases and organs whether in the office or not. Remove the words *cure, treat* and *diagnose* from your vocabulary. In addition, I also advise you not to refer to those you see as *patients,* but as *clients.* That's what licensed health practitioners do and we do not want to be confused with them.

What to Legally Call Yourself

If you are a naturopath and did not go to one of the seven medical/naturopathic schools, but possess a degree or diploma that says you are a doctor of naturopathy; you are an *unlicensed naturopath*. That means if you live in a state that licenses naturopaths, you must be sure you do not represent yourself as a naturopathic physician, so you should not use the ND designation.[7] State clearly in your literature that you are an unlicensed health practitioner and have your clients sign a form saying they understand. As far as what to call yourself, you may consider the titles, holistic health consultant or natural health practitioner. It could also be, traditional naturopath or naturopathic practitioner. Some states are stricter than others when it comes to the word "naturopathy" allowing no variation of the word at all. You must check the laws of your state on that issue. Contrary to what many people think, the word "doctor" is not regulated (It actually means teacher, if you can believe that). The issue is that you do not represent yourself as a licensed physician.

If you are a traditional naturopath living in a non-licensing state, you can usually call yourself a naturopathic doctor, doctor of naturopathy and use the designation ND after your name, unless you live in a state that outlaws naturopathy altogether such as South Carolina and Tennessee. If you are a

---

[7] Rumor has it that the designation for Naturopathic Physicians in California will change to NMD, which stands for Naturopathic Medical Doctor, and ND will be reserved for Traditional Naturopaths. But as of this writing, it has not happened. So, if you live in California, call yourself something else

PhD, it's perfectly legal to call yourself "Dr. So and So" no matter where you live, although the title is usually reserved for medical doctors and chiropractors. Once again, you must be sure you establish that you are not a physician and that none of your services are for treating, diagnosing or curing.

You cannot call yourself a *dietician* as it is also a regulated designation. You must also be careful of the word *nutritionist.* In certain states such as Ohio and Florida, the term is regulated, so if you live there, you would not call yourself a naturopathic nutritionist. Florida also has restrictions on using the word *counselor* and *consultant.* In that case, you may want to consider calling yourself a "natural health educator." But, no matter what you call yourself, what your credential or where you graduated from, you must place your diploma along with your business license in plain sight.

If you are an animal naturopath, you have a lot of leeway as to what to call yourself. You can call yourself a *doctor of animal health*, a *doctor of animal naturopathy, naturopathic animal consultant,* etc. Stay away from the word *veterinarian.* You do not want to be confused with doctors of veterinarian medicine [DVM]. Just like a naturopath for humans, you will not prescribe, diagnose, treat, etc. And you will have pet-owners sign release forms stating that they understand this fact, and that you are not a DVM.

If this all sounds tedious and annoying, well, that's because it is. But don't throw your hands up in frustration and whatever you do, don't get spooked. Always be aware that you have a right to be in the natural health field. No state can prohibit you from *educating* the public concerning proper eating habits, rest, stress reduction, exercise, detoxing methods, etc. Ordinary citizens who focus on the prevention of illness have the right with or without medical degrees and licenses, to set up businesses that educate the public on matters of natural health. Now it is true that in some states such as Florida and Ohio, you must be under the auspices of a licensed health professional in order to consult. But no license is required to guide and instruct others on health and wellness. Only physicians, dieticians, chiropractors, acupuncturists, naturopathic physicians, and osteopaths, and in some states, homeopathic physicians, have governing boards to whom they must answer. We do not and that's a good thing! Just be cognizant of the areas you must avoid which are: (1) disease diagnosis, (2) administering or prescribing X-Rays, (3) advising discontinuance of physician-prescribed medication, (4) cures, remedies or therapies (anything falling under prescribing, including natural cures and dietary treatments), (5) invasive procedures (such as drawing blood or IVs), (6) surgery, (7) manipulations (such as chiropractic or osteopathic), and (8) representing yourself as a physician.

A Visit from the State Medical Board

If your State Medical Board pays you a visit, it will be because someone has reported you, maybe a competitor, a disgruntled client or just someone who would like you "outta there." But, the Board must investigate all reports and they must tell you who filed the complaint. Be polite, calm and cooperative, but make it very clear that you know the law. Also, know that the State Medical Board must meet with you on *your* terms. If you want to meet with them outside your office or in another public place, that's your right. Bring two or three witnesses and an unconcealed recording device, informing them you will be recording the interview for educational purposes. People are far more careful as to what they say if they know they are being recorded. I am not trying to scare you, but there is always a possibility you could be reported, so you need to know what to do should it happen. However, if you are operating within your legal boundaries, you will have no problems and nothing to fear, as your State Medical Board will be able to charge you with nothing.

Our concern as natural health consultants is that we guide our clients in learning how to obtain optimal health through lifestyle modifications, exercise and stress reduction. You will *teach* the clients; therefore leaving the responsibility concerning their *own* health where it belongs, with them. Now, I am well aware that the average person who comes to see a natural health consultant normally does so because he/she is looking for a cure for a specific disease or condition. The only difference between you and a medical doctor in their eyes, is your "cure" will be one with no side effects. That mindset is to be expected because that is what has been ingrained in

Americans for the last 100 years. But, it is up to you as a natural health practitioner to change that way of thinking and show them how to improve health. If you truly understand and believe that the majority of health problems are due to toxicity, malnourishment, deficiency of water, lack of exercise and a negative mindset, then you will have no trouble staying within your legal parameters. If not, you will always be tempted to operate in the disease industry by offering cures, diagnosing, and other regulated practices, placing you in violation of the law. Not to mention you will be doing your clients a great disservice by failing to teach the natural health principles that they so desperately need. Never forget that people need you. I said this earlier: if the so-called established health industry in this nation were doing its job, the public wouldn't need our profession. Be aware of your boundaries, but go forth with clarity and confidence.

Malpractice Insurance

Although, as holistic health consultants, we will never manipulate, prescribe, draw blood, inject needles or do anything else considered invasive, you're going to need to acquire insurance. It's like any insurance, you don't like paying for it, but you don't want to be without it either. We all know how sue-happy Americans are. Think about this: when a person starts a health program he can often experience detoxing symptoms ranging from headaches, body aches and fatigue, to pronounced symptoms such as nausea, vomiting and even fainting. You tell people this can happen, but they usually don't get it. So what if your client experiences some extremes reactions, gets scared and decides to sue? Or, what if a he has an episode that has nothing to do with your program at all, but happens to be seeing you at the same time? I know of a natural health practitioner who counseled a woman with a medically diagnosed heart problem. She was not under the care of any physician at the time, her blood pressure was normal and she had signed a form authorizing the practitioner to begin a program. A few weeks later while at a family gathering, she suffered a heart attack and died. The family actually considered that the natural health program she'd been on might have contributed to her death. They did listen to reason however, and no action was ever taken. *But, they thought about it.* It may have never won in a court of law, but if you had a similar situation occur and it was pursued, it could cost you money, time and stress. And just the notoriety could put you out of business. Malpractice insurance is inexpensive, easy to obtain and worth it for just the peace of mind. Get it. Your home or car insurance agency should be able to help as to what companies are available, but I have listed some in the appendix.

Naming Your Business

Whatever you choose to name your business, it must conform to the to legal parameters as discussed. After you understand all the ramifications, start the process by thinking of names that will best convey to the public the service you provide. Key words to use will be *wellness, holistic health, natural health,* etc. Keep it simple and easy to remember. My advice is to use no more than three words total including your last name. You can aim for something catchy, but be careful. You do not want to come across as cutesy or you will be viewed as a non-professional. *The Boiling Cauldron Herbologist* comes to mind, as does *Pin Cushion Acupuncture Services* (yes, these names were actually considered). Health professionals do not make a joke out of their vocation. At some point soon after opening your practice, you will want to incorporate as a business entity. As incorporation is a complex issue, we will not discuss it here. There are many fine books on the subject and you will eventually need to learn about the process. But keep incorporation in mind when thinking about what to name your business.

Assessment Systems

In order to help someone you must find out to the best of your ability what is wrong with them. We're not talking about naming a specific disease; we're talking about getting to the root of a problem. If you don't and just help them relieve a symptom, you're not helping them gain health. To determine a core-issue, you'll need some sort of an assessment system to help you find out what it is. Let me illustrate:

I once had a client who came to me complaining she couldn't sleep. She lay awake night after night for almost two years. She tried every natural aid from valerian to melatonin to tryptophan and nothing helped. In desperation, she finally resorted to medication, but didn't want to be dependent on it, because it made her groggy and listless. Through my assessment system, I was able to find that that there was an imbalance in her endocrine function, primarily with her thyroid and adrenals. I took it a step further; discerning that what was throwing them off was food sensitivities, especially where sugar and wheat products were concerned. I also determined that she had a pronounced yeast/bacteria imbalance in her GI tract. I recommended the appropriate, health-optimizing supplements along with a proper diet, and within two weeks, she was sleeping through the night without medication.

In order to help this woman I had to know more information other than she just couldn't sleep. I had to try to figure out *why*. She had already tried the standard natural supplements for insomnia with no success. She knew there was a deeper problem that eluded her (and her medical doctor). I used four assessment techniques to decipher her core issues: a symptom survey/client information form, metabolic urinalysis, electro-dermal screening, and deltoid kinesiology. By using all four, I was able to get a multi-faceted picture as to what her issues were.

There are systems out there that are designed to help you get to a core issue that trust, me, you will not be able to find by a health questionnaire, alone. An intake form is mandatory, because you can discover what the client is concerned with and what they are feeling, but there's a good chance you'll miss things that are not immediately obvious. And also, your client's answers are going to be very subjective. You will want a system that's objective, repeatable and accurate, along with being easy for the client to understand. It will also need to have identifiable and measurable markers allowing tangible progress to be tracked.

From a marketing point of view, a system able to furnish printed charts and graphs is highly desirable. Americans love charts and graphs. They'll view you and what you do as more credible if you can provide them with such. Remember, a great deal of what we do is about perception. When people go to a medical doctor for a test, they normally get some sort of a printout. They may not understand a thing on it, but at least they'll have one showing the results. And that is what your clients will want from you:documented results — just as their MD gives them — so they can compare one visit to the next. It doesn't have to come from a system that involves expensive, ultra-high-tech equipment that takes an engineer to assemble. It just should be something the client can see and take home. If it can be computer-generated, great. If not, it just needs to be professional and easy to understand. Fortunately for the alternative health practitioner, there are a number of excellent, accurate and user-friendly systems that fit the bill.

As a side note, I suggest that in your repertoire you use methods that are not too "out there." Now, I know that what may be "out there" today could be mainstream tomorrow. Chiropractic and acupuncture are examples. But, you don't want to use methods that are so esoteric they'll scare people away. For example, there is a man in my town who practices using a divining rod, like you used to see when people would look for water. He waves it over the body and if it vibrates, it's supposed to mean something. There's also a woman in town who is a "holistic intuitive." She puts her hand on your hand, closes her eyes and concentrates. She then purports to receive information as to what you need, sort of like the famous psychic/healer Edgar Cayce. Whether their methods are effective or not I cannot say, but what I can say is that 99% of the population will never come to see them for a health consultation. One of our biggest challenges is to get the mainstream to see that alternative medicine is not voodoo or hocus-pocus, but viable and necessary. You will not do that by choosing strange and possibly controversial techniques that maybe one out of 10,000 are going to go for.

My suggestion is to find a well-known system within the alternative health community that resonates with you, and then do your research. Find other practitioners who are using it and talk to them. Some things to think about while deciding are: how much time, effort and money will it take to learn the system? Does the company offer adequate support concerning technical and customer service issues? Is their training effective? Does the company make available upgrades and improvements on a regular basis? Do they have good marketing materials? Is it affordable for you at this particular time? Can the clients easily chart their progress? And of course, will clients see it as valid?

Once you find the systems or devices you want to use, become the best at them you can possibly be. You want to be a master, not a dabbler or a dilettante. Attend all the seminars, watch all the videos and become the consummate professional. Practice, practice, practice on your friends, relatives, anyone. In the beginning, you'll need to do this to learn and acquire competence. When you are competent, you will acquire confidence and with that, your clients will come. The following are a few of some of the more common assessment systems and devices that alternative practitioners are using, with some commentary. Specific companies with web addresses will be listed in the appendix. Just be sure that whatever system you use, you make clear to each client that none of these devices is for diagnosing any disease or condition. They are for detecting nutritional imbalances and deficiencies so an appropriate program can be developed.

Electro-Dermal Screening is an energetic assessment where a machine is used to produce a tiny electrical current, too small to be detected by the client. The testing device sends a current through a probe, completing a low-voltage electrical circuit. On a computer screen or by using a needle on a gauge, a number will appear indicating if body-system meridians are out of balance. These devices can be used to find substance sensitivities, organ weakness, parasites, heavy metal intoxication, dietary intolerances, pesticide burden, nutrient deficiencies, and more. There are some devices that have the frequencies of herbs and other supplements loaded into the apparatus, so you can create your own homeopathic remedies.

More and more practitioners are using these devices worldwide. Some are more user-friendly than others are, but all of them have software enabling the client to take home a printed graph where he or she can over time, chart their progress.

Heart Rate Variability Testing (HRV) is a computer-based system designed for quantitative assessment of the autonomic nervous system. It measures functionality of the parasympathetic and sympathetic nervous system by analyzing heart waves. It's quick, user-friendly and an effective way of determining overall physical fitness.

Muscle Testing, also known as Reflex Nutritional Assessment (RNA), Contact Reflex Analysis (CRA), Deltoid Kineseology, (DK) Nutritional Response Testing (NRT) and O-Ring Testing (ORT), is an energetic testing modality that uses the practitioner instead of a machine as the vehicle for assessing a client. The practitioner places his hand on a point of the body corresponding with an organ or organ system and applies pressure. At the same time, the practitioner pushes down on the topside of the wrist of an outstretched arm. If the practitioner is using the O-Ring method, he/she tries to open a ring made by the thumb and index finger. If the organ or system is in balance, the arm or fingers will stay locked. If it is stressed, the arm or fingers will give way. This method can also be used to determine what substances can either weaken or strengthen the organ or system, by placing the substances on the body. There are a few drawbacks to this technique. First, although this method is gaining more acceptance all the time, it may seem strange to people. Second, there are no computer printouts for the client to visually monitor any progress. Third and very important, this method can be highly subjective. There are many outside factors that can easily affect the outcome

The good points of muscle testing are that there are no machines needed, it can be done anywhere and if done correctly, is a highly effective way of deciphering core issues that aren't immediately obvious. I once had a client whom every time I muscle tested her, would be weak on the thyroid point. I suggested there was some sort of problem, but she dismissed it because her physician had recently given her a blood test and told her that her thyroid was fine. She stopped seeing me soon afterwards, but two years later, she called to tell me she had thyroid cancer. According to her, I was the *only* practitioner who said that there could be an issue with her thyroid. No one else had detected it. That is the beauty of muscle testing and most energetic devices. You can detect the direction a person is headed health-wise, before they become symptomatic. That is a big, big deal.

One important factor when it comes to muscle or O-ring testing: the tester must be in good health. You can't cheat and be really good at this mode of assessing. If you are in poor physical health, you will not pick up issues in those who are healthier than you. You must live what you teach.

Metabolic Urinalysis is a system whereby you obtain a person's urine and analyze for metabolic by-products, revealing issues such as adrenal stress, calcium adequacy, bone loss, digestion, overall glucose, electrolyte balance, free-radical activity, urine weight, ammonia levels and other valuable information in determining a health profile. In my opinion, this should be a part of any practice, gathering biochemical information as well as that obtained by a symptom survey and energetic methods. It is completely objective, easily explainable and understandable to the client. And with some companies you as the practitioner, can be trained to do the testing yourself, not incurring an additional expense for the client.

Sclerology is the study of the red lines in the white of the eyes and how they relate to stress patterns in a person's health. The physical characteristics of the sclera, such as shape and location of markings, can be related to systemic health. The sclera reveals a great number of disease processes and is capable of showing data indicating past and current health concerns. Sclerology requires no clinical tools and is an objective, non-invasive method of evaluation. I personally have had sclerology readings and have found them very accurate. This method, in my opinion, shows great promise in the field of natural health.

Voice Assessment functions on the principle that the human voice is used not only as a medium of communication, but also exhibits frequencies of the physical body, mind and emotions. By taking a voiceprint, you can determine which notes are out of balance, corresponding to organs and emotions that are out of balance. You can then use sound therapy along with nutrition, herbs homeopathy or whatever you choose to balance and strengthen the systems in question. I personally love this technique. It just seems to work. It's fast, accurate and relatively inexpensive to learn and acquire the equipment. And you have a computer-generated graph for the client.

Hair Analysis processes and analyzes a hair sample checking for mineral deficiencies and heavy metal toxicity. Hair is normally sent to a lab for results but there are some kits where you the practitioner can do the testing. Advantages are it's objective and easily understood.

These are some assessment techniques available. Most of them require credentials for purchase, but not all. Whatever methods you choose, become a master at them. You can never become overly proficient at your craft. The good practitioners are always attending seminars and fine-tuning. You always need to stay current on the latest information concerning your profession and the various methods you use.

I have one more comment to make on the subject of assessment systems: it's possible that while enrolled in your natural health school, you were told that there are many successful practitioners out there with viable practices who use nutritional counseling alone. That may well be possible, but in all my years in the field, I have never met one. The ones who are making it work use some sort of analysis system to find core issues. You have to, you really do.

Forms

You will need a number of forms for your consulting business. First, you must have an authorization form signed by the client allowing you to proceed with your services. In it you should clearly state that you are *not* a medical doctor and you do not treat, diagnose, or cure disease. You will also need their permission to use your assessment methods on them. *Never, ever, consult with anyone without a signed authorization form(s).* Any time you collect money from anyone you counsel, including phone consultations, you must have one. If the client is a minor, make sure a parent signs it. Sample forms are found in the appendix.

In addition to the consent forms, I also include a document from the Better Business Bureau where the client signs an agreement stating that should he/she ever want to pursue legal action against me, it would go to arbitration and not to a court of law. Seriously consider including this document, because the truth is, *you could still end up in court even with a signed authorization.* Not so with this particular form, as it is legally binding. Contact your local BBB office for more information as to how to obtain one for your practice.

Symptom/Health Survey

You need to have a health questionnaire for a couple of reasons. First, in order to develop a nutritional program you'll need to get information from clients about their state of health. It doesn't need to be long and complex, but it should be designed in a way that you can easily determine what they are doing and how they are feeling on a daily basis. You'll need to know such things as eating and sleeping patterns, medications, surgeries, supplements, emotional health, if they have pets, etc. You should convey to the client that you are primarily interested in what their lifestyle is and what their choices have been, *long-term*. I once had a client who was overweight, sick and gray. In the section on life-style habits, she described a diet and exercise program that would put me to shame. When questioned about it she told me that she had found the program in a book and had been *trying* to do it for the last week. As the practitioner, I failed to explain effectively that I needed to know what she'd been doing consistently in the past, not just the past week. My mistake was thinking that she and all potential clients would understand that point. They don't. So be sure you are very clear as to what kind of information you need. Also, be sure the client understands that there is no judgment concerning past choices.

On your initial questionnaire, you always want your clients to be very specific as to what is their most important health issue, as this will be the thing you will work on first. Even if it isn't a core issue, meaning it is a symptom of a core issue, you should consider handling it as soon as possible. For example, I once had a man who came to me because he had high blood pressure. He also had type II diabetes, but his main concern was his blood pressure. He wanted to reduce it so his doctor would reduce his medication. Now I know that in a diabetic, high blood pressure is usually the result of impaired pancreatic function. But in the first months, I only worked on his blood pressure. You may ask, "Why didn't you work on the pancreas, which was obviously the core issue?" The answer is because blood pressure was his main concern. Yes, eventually we addressed his endocrine function, but initially I worked on getting his blood pressure down, because *that is what he came to see me about.* You must try to help the client with what's most important to them if you can; the reason being that unless you have truly dedicated clients who really understand that it can take time to eradicate symptoms, they will usually quit the program and stop seeing you after about a month if they don't feel or see any progress. Never forget people in America have a drug mentality; it's what they've been indoctrinated with. So we have to be sensitive to this while understanding that we will eventually address the core issue. But we will also always make sure our clients understand that symptomatic relief through meds is not health, and in order for them to experience true and lasting improvement, *it's going to take time.*

Another very important reason for the questionnaire is to find out what, if any, medications they are taking. A person may have hives, headaches, constipation, diarrhea and fatigue, which may appear to be nutritional deficiencies or toxicity. But what's really happening is that these symptoms are drug related and a nutritional program alone will not alleviate them. If that's the case, it is *always* between the client and his physician to decide when to reduce or eliminate any medication.

I usually email or snail-mail the required forms ahead of time so clients can have them filled out before they arrive. I get all contact information on their first call to my office and as a side note, I always ask who referred them. I never give an appointment indiscriminately. I always ask how they heard about me. They must have a name of someone I recognize or a location where I either lectured or am known, such as health store, or a workout facility, before I'll give a consultation. This is to keep undesirables and possible troublemakers out. Also, do not forget that on the first contact, you should make it clear that you are not a medical doctor, but a natural health consultant. Sample health questionnaire forms are in the appendix.

Report of Findings

The next form you'll need is the Report of Findings (ROF). The ROF is a form that you will give to your clients detailing the results of all assessments you have used. It needs to be clear, direct and free of practitioner-jargon. In addition, I advise having a separate form for each test, for the sake of clarity. You will also include any printouts generated from any machines you have used to assess your clients (more on that later).

Tailored Health Program

You will also prepare an invidualized, tailored health program, resultant of your assessment(s). Have it on a separate sheet from the ROF. It should include which supplements they need, dosages, when to take them and any other special instructions. If applicable, note contraindications with any OTC or physician-prescribed medications. You will give this information on a specific office visit) more on that when we cover how to structure appointments).

Be sure all your forms are organized, readable and easily accessible. Make your client notes clear, concise and complete. It is always possible you will be called upon to produce them. I also advise avoiding the mention of any disease in your notes that your client may have. There is always a chance that could be construed as practicing medicine. This may seem overly cautious, but you want to be certain there is never any question concerning the legalities of your practice.

The Right Office Location

Finding a suitable space depends on what you can afford. I recommend getting an office in town, but with rents these days, that may not be feasible when you first start out. Many practitioners begin by using a room in their home and then, when they can afford it, move to an office. If that's what you must do, you need to be mindful of a few things, the first and foremost being professionalism. If you work at home, you may not be viewed as credible as someone with an office. That may not seem fair, but that's the way it is so you must be as professional as you possibly can. Think of driving by houses with cheesy signs on the lawn, advertising psychics or beauty parlors inside. You want to avoid that perception at all costs!

First, you will need to have a separate room, with a bathroom nearby, preferably as far away from the rest of the house as possible. Keep all your related books, tables, testing kits, and forms in the room. Have it neat and orderly with nothing else in it except that which pertains to your practice. When you are in session, have your house quiet with no other family members present unless they are assisting you. Remember, clients are used to doctor's offices with waiting areas, receptionists and examining rooms. Your work area doesn't need to be sterile and hospital-like, but it needs to appear orderly and suited for the purpose for which your clients are coming to see you. If they come to your house and the dog is barking, the kids are running around and the TV is blaring, they will most likely not return. I know I wouldn't. Ideally, your space would be one with a separate entrance, perhaps a redone basement or den with an outside pathway to the door, away from your living quarters. Just be sure it is workable and efficient. You'll have to work extra-hard to project a professional image if you're working at home, but it can be done. And if you want to put a sign outdoors, have it be smallish and understated!

The other option would be to rent an office in a business area. I recommend trying to find one with others who are in the health field such as chiropractors, acupuncturists, massage therapists, physical therapists, nurse practitioners and even medical doctors if you know they wouldn't be antagonistic to what you do. Call them and ask if they have any rooms available for rent. Features to look for in a center are: is the location in a good area? Does it have Internet access? How about a fax and copy machine? Is there a meeting room where you could hold lectures to build your practice? This feature will be very important to you, so have it high on your list of priorities. Would you have access to the building if you wanted to make special evening and weekend appointments? Is it secure and in a safe area? Is it noisy or quiet? Are you comfortable with the other practitioners and/or tenants in the center? Is the landlord someone you can trust? How long would the lease be for? Get all your questions answered then once you find a place that suits you, negotiate the rent if it seems too high. Remember, most property owners would rather have an occupied room than an empty one.

Another item to consider; would you have a receptionist/assistant that would make appointments for you?If you're in a space that has other health professionals, see if that would be possible as this will really help with your professional image. If the receptionist could also collect your client fees, that would be excellent. It's a psychological thing, but you need to have someone other than yourself taking the money when clients pay for your services. Eventually you will want to get your own personally trained assistant who will act as a client liaison/advocate. He/she will also be answering your phone, monitoring inventory, doing the ordering, helping with marketing, and assisting clients with questions about their programs. If you cannot afford to pay an assistant when you are first starting out, try to find someone you can take on as an apprentice. Contact the school you attended and see if there is a natural health student in the area who may be interested. Getting an assistant will be paramount to your success.

Here's something a very resourceful practitioner in Texas did: he bought a used RV and made it into an office. He has power, water, a restroom, storage, everything he needs. Most of his clients work at two locations, so he drives the RV to their respective parking lots and meets with them during the day.

When he's finished, he drives home and parks his "office" in his driveway. It works for him!

I do not recommend making house visits as your main way of meeting with clients. Although it may seem like a good idea because you wouldn't have any overhead, it can be problematic. First, you'll have to lug all your equipment with you. If you have an examining table, testing kits and/or assessment devices, you'll have to load them in your car, unload them and then load them up again at each appointment. Secondly, unless you really know your client, you don't know what kind of a situation you could be walking into. I know of a practitioner who made a home visit to a house that was filthy. After leaving she had to literally wipe down and sterilize *all* her equipment. Had she had another appointment right after, she would have had to cancel it because there was no way she could have used her equipment on another person without cleaning it first. There could also be distractions such as children, spouses, ringing phones, and other situations over which you have no control. And most importantly, going to a place that is unfamiliar is bound to be stressful on some level to you as a practitioner. You do not want to be stressed out when meeting with a client, especially if you use energetic modes of assessing. It could potentially affect the outcomes.

Find a place that is you're comfortable with. Take your time and find the right one, because it's where you are going to be spending a lot of your time. Don't rush and take the first space you come across if it's not right. You might regret it if you do.

Keeping Records

Once you find your workspace, you will need to have a filing system where you keep all your records. Mine is, for the most part, paperless, but there are some items that require hard copies. Client files, informational handouts, master files of all required forms, tax records and promotional info are some that come to mind. Being organized and having easily accessible information will make your life so much easier. As far as your accounting goes, there are many software programs you can purchase enabling you to monitor inventory, expenses, income, etc. In the beginning you probably won't need an extensive, in-depth program, so you may want to consider using something like Microsoft Excel or Numbers. You should be able to create a system that will cover your basic needs.

As far as taxes go, be sure you keep a really good handle on them. I suggest you open a separate account and make tax-deposits on a weekly basis. And here's the key: *don't touch the account until it's time to pay them!* I've known a few entrepreneurs that were lax on this issue and it caused them major headaches. So be disciplined about this and you won't have unnecessary tax problems.

Marketing

Once you are ready to start consulting with clients, you'll need to market yourself. Obviously you'll need business cards, brochures, flyers and postcards. These items must be professional, but you don't need to spend a fortune on them. I've always used *Vistaprint.com*. You can choose from pre-designed templates and really get a great deal, or you can design them yourselves. They offer quality, professional products at an excellent price. Just be sure all your marketing materials clearly explain your services in a simple and concise manner.

Next, you need to get out and let people know you are available. That is called *marketing* and is one the most important aspects of creating a successful practice, yet one the most neglected. I'm going to spend some time on this subject because if you're going to be successful, you *must* learn to do it effectively. I know practitioners who have gone to school, gotten the equipment, rented an office and just sat, waiting for people to show up. Maybe they were applying the "if you build it, they will come" thing from the movie *Field of Dreams*. Read this and understand; ***it is not enough to be good at what you do, even if you're really good.*** You're going to have to get out there and tell everyone you're here. As much as you might hate it, you're going to have to get out and be a salesperson, at least for a while anyway. But the good news is, there is no shortage of potential clients. Americans spend millions of dollars each year in the alternative health field. They're looking for answers. They're looking for *you*. There are folks out there who want your help and will gladly pay your fees; you just need to know who they are, and how to find them.

The first weekend after I moved into my office, I had a grand opening party (which you too will want to do). I called everyone I knew and invited them — friends, family, co-workers, business associates, everyone. I handed out flyers; put up posters and did all I could to try to get people there. A sales representative from a supplement company brought his marketing materials and the food. For the presentation I got up and gave a brief talk about why natural health, and then did a muscle-testing demonstration. Fifty people attended and 10 signed up for consultations Most of the people who attended were women, although I invited men as well. All the sign-ups were women. And that's the first thing about marketing as a natural health consultant I want you to understand: your target market is women.

Your Main Market

Women in the 35-55-age bracket, usually married and with children, at any given time will comprise about 98% of your practice. As women almost always determine what enters the household concerning health and nutrition, you will want to gear all your business-building efforts towards them. Forget marketing to men. Not that I have anything against them, it's just

84

that usually they don't make good nutritional clients. Chiropractic patients, yes, but most just don't seem to get the natural health thing, especially when it comes to diet. You can also forget senior citizens 75 and above. Now that may sound harsh, but trust me on this one. Most of these folks are like zombies when it comes to their MDs, even if they are on 20 meds a day. They'll do anything their doctors tell them. They're indoctrinated into the medical system like no other segment of the population. With that being said, however, understand that this will not be the case forever. The baby-boomers are becoming senior citizens and they are the biggest economic force in history. They have spent their health acquiring wealth, and unfortunately they will be spending their wealth to trying to regain their health. So fairly soon they will be a huge market.

I also strongly advise that as a new practitioner, you stay away from people with catastrophic illnesses. Those who have them usually need to be monitored by physicians and almost always need more than what we can offer. Resist the urge to believe that nutrition alone is the answer to every health condition under the sun. It's not. Always remember that what we are looking for are the people who know they are on a downward slide and feel that something is just not quite right. We are *not* looking for people who have serious, life-threatening illnesses and are coming to us as their last hope. Why? Because odds are you will not be able to help them, your confidence will be shaken and you could even open yourself up to lawsuits. We want people who are looking to avoid the medical nightmare, not those who are hopelessly in it.

Creating a Niche/Specialization

There are many naturopaths and alternative health consultants who function as general practitioners and do very well. But the ones who seem to do the best are the specialists. The more I study what's happening in the field of alternative medicine and health-care in general, the more convinced I am that specializing is a great idea. I believe that when it comes to health, people would prefer to see a health-care provider that is an expert on their problem. Think about it; with most fields there are areas of specialization. This is certainly true in the medical field, but this applies to other fields as well. In dentistry, there are orthodontists. In cosmetology there are those are hair-colorists. In the fitness field, there are aerobic instructors, Pilates instructors, etc. Is there one area of study or concern that appeals to you more than all the others? I know an extremely successful practitioner whose main area of expertise is hormonal issues. Women from all over the US seek his services. Other burgeoning fields are autism, pediatric natural health, endocrine issues, detoxification and as mentioned previously, animal health. Let's face it; you can't be an expert on everything. Yes, in the beginning as a new practitioner you will be learning about all areas of natural health and all of it will be intriguing. But as your practice evolves, seriously consider finding that one area that you are most passionate about, and really focus your energy there.

Who to Call

You can start by calling on the PTA, YMCA, women's networking groups, social groups, MOPS (Mother's of Preschoolers), and church groups for example, and ask to be a featured speaker. My experience has been that these organizations are always looking for lecturers and love it when anyone speaks on natural health. Pick subjects that are relevant, easy to explain and appeal to women. The hormone issue is very hot right now (No pun intended!). So is weight loss, and anti-aging.

Lectures and seminars are going to be a big part of developing your business, so make peace with that fact. If you're afraid to stand up in front of people, have never done any public speaking, or just have no idea how to do it, contact Toastmasters Inc., a national group with local chapters. They will teach you how to be an effective public speaker. If there aren't groups where you live, which would be unusual unless you really live in the sticks, purchase a book on the subject and start practicing. Call on your friends, family members, anyone who will listen and offer constructive feedback. You don't have to be the consummate professional; you just need to know the basics.

Lecturing

After you've picked your subject, you'll want to name your lecture in a way that's attention grabbing. To illustrate the point, I once gave a talk at our local health food store called, *How to Be Healthy Naturally*. The content was good, well prepared, and well advertised, but I had a dismal turnout. I gave another soon after named *How to Have Beautiful Skin, The Key to Beauty*. I had standing room only, picked up new clients and made contacts for future speaking engagements. The content of the skin lecture was almost the same as *How to be Healthy Naturally*, but it was just packaged differently. We all want beautiful skin as everyone wants to look good. Remember Billy Crystal impersonating Fernando Lamas on *Saturday Night Live*? "It's not how you feel, it's how you look, dahling." So true. So pick a subject that people want to hear about as a come-on, but focus on what you really want to communicate.

Weight loss is always a good subject as a hook. Stay away from subjects like sexual dysfunction and depression. Most people will not admit they have a problem in those areas even to themselves, let alone in a public setting. And don't bother doing one on stress either. The people who really need it aren't going to show up, they're too stressed out!

And this brings me to another very important point. When you pick a subject to speak on, pick one that you truly want to help clients with. As an example, I never lecture on cancer. I may mention it as a side issue if it's relevant to the subject matter, but I never make it my main topic because I do not want to counsel people with cancer. But I very much enjoy helping women with hormone issues, so I speak on the subject frequently. And so it follows, I have many clients seeking hormonal help. You will attract what you speak on, so be sure it's an area in which you're comfortable.

A couple more things to keep in mind; your talk should be under an hour. A lot of the information you give them may be totally new and you don't want to overwhelm them. They'll turn off if you do. Next, as the attendees will always bombard you with questions, (I always ask them to hold them until the end) keep the answers very general and non-condition-specific. The point of these lectures is to build your practice, not to give away free information. Give them enough just to whet their appetite, making them want more.

Another thing to know: when speaking to an audience, you must not dwell on the negative. Yes, the health picture in America is bad, but resist the urge to portray it as completely horrible. We offer hope and that is what makes us *different* from the medical establishment. We tell them that they *don't* have to be sick, fat, depressed, pain-ridden, and eventually burdensome to their children, ending up in a nursing home. We offer them a way out. I've had more than one client tell me that I was the *only* health-care professional that gave them hope! Therefore, in all your public speaking engagements, newsletters and any endeavor concerning your practice, always come across as positive, enthusiastic and hopeful for the future.

One last comment I'll make about lecturing: always know your audience. I was once invited to speak to a group of guys at a naval base who had failed their physicals and were required to take health-education training. I was a new practitioner, very zealous and very naïve. I prepared a lecture "telling it like it is" that had all sorts of information that this group clearly wasn't ready to hear. Not to mention my delivery was completely annoying. It was a total disaster. So badly did I fail in fact, I actually got hate-calls! If I had just taken the time to think about to whom I was speaking, the outcome could have been different. But instead, I bulldozed forward with no thought as to even why these folks were listening to me in the first place:it was mandatory. It was a painful, humbling experience. So, think about your audience and their threshold to the type of information you'll be giving. Talking about food to some people is almost like talking about religion. So, be careful and tactful.

You will of course, at all your lectures, come prepared with business cards, brochures, and a price list. You may want to consider offering a special discount for anyone who makes an appointment and pays for it right then and there. Be sure and have a sign-in sheet with spaces for name, email and phone contact. That way you can still market to those who don't make appointments immediately.

Start a Natural Health Association

Another way to start getting your name out there is to start a natural health association with you as the president. The goal is public awareness concerning natural health, which will build your business. Find a suitable meeting place (at your office if possible), and give regularly scheduled lectures once a month or so. Email all your clients, friends, family members and have them email *their* friends and family. Put flyers up in churches, health-food stores, beauty salons, anywhere people may be interested in looking and feeling good. Charge a yearly fee that will cover copying costs and other incidentals. Tell the members they can bring guests free of charge for one lecture. Send or email a monthly newsletter to all members covering health topics and anything you might think relevant. You may also want to do recognition blurbs for clients who have lost weight through your counseling, overcome a health challenge, anything that will edify the clients, which in turn will edify you.

Getting Referrals from Professionals

Think about calling on MDs and making them aware you are in business. Don't be intimidated. Some are enlightened as to the importance of natural health principles and will refer out. I know of a practitioner in Connecticut who built a very large practice by doing just that. Give them your brochure along with a description of your services and don't be afraid to ask for referrals. You may also consider calling on chiropractors if they're not incorporating nutrition into their own practice. Some are very happy to know of a professional nutritional consultant they can send their patients to.

Another way I got new clients was to go to the local health food store and give the manager a free health screening. In this, she got to know me and could see how I could help her customers. She then allowed me to put a table up on weekends in the store (free of charge) to advertise my services. Now you may be thinking, wouldn't a health-food-store manager view us as competitors? Not at all. I always send people there for groceries and personal-care products. So, think of what businessperson you may know who may be in a position to help you. How about your hairstylist, manicurist, personal trainer, or gym manager? Offer a free consultation and ask them if they know of others you could help.

The Tupperware Party

Don't laugh. It's one of the best venues for building a clientele. There's a reason why billion-dollar companies like Tupperware® and Mary Kay® use home-parties as a business model. It works. When I had my first few clients, I asked one of them if she would be amenable to inviting some of her friends over and having me give a lecture on natural health. The benefit to her would be a percentage off her next appointment and a discount to any new clients who signed up and paid that night. The hostess prepared light, healthy snacks for her 11 guests. I spoke for about a half and hour, did some simple muscle-testing demonstrations, and then opened it up for questions. I also had my client (the hostess) give a personal testimony as how my program had helped improve her health. It was a lot of fun and I picked up six new clients.

Take a Survey

On a Saturday afternoon have a friend or family member who is supportive of you go down to the local grocery store, Trader Joes, Whole Foods or anywhere people might be open to the natural health message. What they're going to do is stop people (in the parking lot, not in the store) and ask them to take a survey regarding their personal health (which you will have created). People love to talk about themselves, especially where health is concerned. Ask them about *how* and *what* they are feeling. When they tell you how bad they feel, and believe me they will, get them to embellish on it. Get them to think about what serious consequences could occur if their health didn't improve, either to them, their family, financial situation, etc. When they have finished talking, have the survey taker then explain that there is hope, and suggest an appointment. This is how one practitioner I know got his first 30 clients and his business mushroomed from there. His wife took the surveys and the two of them together built a million-dollar-a-year nutritional practice. Your survey-taker will obviously have to be someone who is friendly, pleasant, unafraid of talking to people, and skilled at communication. It cannot be you however, because of the credibility issue. But this is a proven method and it can work.

On the Radio

Talk radio is an excellent way of reaching many people at one time. Find out what local shows broadcast in your area and call them to ask if they'd like to have you as a guest. What you should do is: compose a set of questions you want the host to ask you along with your general responses. Include interesting, attention-grabbing facts that will resonate with the public. As an example, I often tell people about how cruciferous vegetables such as broccoli and cauliflower break down large, estrogen molecules helping reduce breast cancer. People love hearing this kind of information. You will also want to include anecdotes and stories as to what natural healing can do. But whatever you do, *do not* turn the show into a discussion on the evils of the established medical system! To many people, that would be a complete turn-off.

Networking

Many entrepreneurs join networking groups where they can interact with other professionals seeking to make their services known. There are a number of groups out there with local chapters such as Business Network International (BNI) and the Chamber of Commerce. There are obviously advantages to joining, but some require a big time commitment and naturally there is a fee. Here's what you can do to avoid the cost and assume the control if you are hardcore committed and a go-getter: start a networking group yourself, with no fee. If you have a meeting/lecture room in your office suite this will work great: hold a meeting once or twice a month around lunchtime for one hour and 15 minutes. The first 15 minutes people will socialize and network. The next 20 minutes, have participants stand up and give a one-minute commercial about who they are and what they do (keep the group under 15 to stay on schedule). The remaining time will be spent with you presenting whatever it is you want to present; a power point presentation, a lecture on natural health, etc. Make sure your guests know the agenda before they arrive so there will be no confusion. And don't forget to tell participants to bring their lunches. Try to get a different group of people at every meeting, which shouldn't be too hard. Most business people are happy to advertise to anyone, especially if it's free. You may have to invest in a screen and projector, but with the new business coming in, these items should pay for themselves quickly. Or you can rent them from a business-office store.

If you don't have a suitable lecture-room at your office, ask around and try to find one. I do not advise using a restaurant even though many have separate meeting rooms. There are too many distractions. I've tried this a few times and it just doesn't work very well. Banks, insurance companies and larger real estate offices often have rooms that would work. Try and persuade them to let you use their rooms at no charge, pointing out the fact that by doing so, it'd be free advertising for them.

If you're not up to the task of starting and maintaining your own networking group, then by all means, join one that is already established. The point is get out there and network. Word of mouth referrals are what you want, and professional, structured groups are an excellent way to get your name out.

DreamTeam 100

Another free networking idea is called the "DreamTeam 100 Concept." This looks cool. The goal is to get a group of 100 professionals that will generate referrals to each other. Here's how to start: make a list of professional people who would like to advertise their services. You may not know 100, but you probably know 20 or 30, so start there. Call or snail-mail these folks and ask them for names of other professionals. Tell them you're compiling a list of 100 people to network with. When you get that list, call those on it and get more names. Do this until you get 100. When you get all of them, you send a letter saying something like this:

Dear Mary:
Wouldn't it be great if we both knew ALL of the best professionals to refer our clients to for WHATEVER need they had? I was looking through my files the other day and I figure that I know about 50 other professionals; everything from chiropractors to divorce attorneys. And naturally, I refer my clients to these other professionals, including you! I've prepared a list of the 50 best professionals I know, and have included a copy of it with this letter: It's part of a process called the "DreamTeam 100". I hope it comes in handy for you and your clients should they need a professional resource, as it's sort of like a private rolodex. But as you can see, I only have 50 names, and within 30 days, the goal is to reach a full 100 or more. Are you willing to help?
All you need to do is to fill in about 10 or 15 blanks of professionals that you know, that I do not. That will get them on this list, and when my list is full at 100, I'll send you – and them – an updated copy. My goal is to have a professional resource for virtually

ANY need that my clients might have. I thought this DreamTeam 100 was a great way to build this resource and offer something to share with you and the soon-to-be other 99 professionals in my network. Looking forward to hearing from you!"
Sincerely, (your name)

What business professional *wouldn't* want to be on this list? Seems to me everyone would want in! Spend a day doing this single marketing strategy and the support-work involved and this could be a real winner!

Lunch and Learn

Lunch and Learn is a program where a professional comes in to a corporation and gives a seminar. As the name implies, the seminars take place during lunchtime, lasting for about an hour and a half. A third-party organization finds and books the seminar. The goal is for the presenter to reach prospective clients who will come and hear him/her speak.

The positive aspect of a Lunch and Learn service is that you don't have to do the marketing. The company does it for you, choosing corporations best suited for your presentation. They can also provide you with the lecture material. Some companies also offer business coaching and lecturing techniques as part of the package.

This can be a very effective way to get clients. The drawback is Lunch and Learn services are usually very expensive and may be cost-prohibitive to the beginning practitioner. But if you can afford it, it could be well worth the investment. Many chiropractors use the service. Find one and ask which company he/she uses. You can also google "Lunch and Learn" and see what comes up, but a personal referral would be best.

Teachers and Child-Care Professionals

Teachers and day-care workers are an excellent market. They're always sick as they're in constant contact with children. Go to day-care centers, kindergartens, elementary, middle and high schools and ask if you can distribute your brochures to all teachers and staff members. Ask if you can put them in the break rooms and in their mailboxes. With your brochure, consider adding a flyer with information on the importance of bolstering the immune system. Some supplement companies have flyers already made up as part of their marketing materials. Contact the sales rep or call them directly. Most will give them to you free or charge a minimal cost.

The Internet

I'm often asked about the Internet and how to use it to build a natural health consulting business. I have a website describing my services as I know it is a must for any business owner today. I do use email to notify my client base, concerning upcoming lectures, events, etc. I use *ConstantContact.com*, an excellent service offering professional emails at great prices. But, I do not send spam promoting myself to strangers, and at this juncture, don't try to increase my numbers using the web. But, things are changing. When the first edition of this book came out, social networking was mainly for personal connecting.

Not anymore. Facebook, Twitter and Linkedin are now considered legitimate and necessary marketing venues for many businesses. But, I still think that using the Internet as your main marketing campaign would be a mistake. This is a personal business and you still must use personal means to build your clientele. *VistaPrint* and *GoDaddy* have beginning websites for excellent prices. Then when you can afford it, you may want to consider hiring a professional web designer to build one for you.

As far as what to put on your site, you will want to outline your services, provide your bio-info, hours of operation, FAQs, links and other information that will help your prospective clients understand who you are and what you do. Obviously be sure it is free of typos, grammatical errors, etc

These are just some ideas as to how to get started. If you're creative, you can probably think of many more. As you can tell, I favor a grass-roots approach when trying to find clients. There are practitioners who advocate going to the administrators of hospitals, HMOs, and other well-established health care agencies, believing that the time is right for them to officially generate referrals for the non-licensed health care professional. I have not found this to be the case. The overwhelming majority of these organizations is still controlled by the medical system, and will not deviate from that influence, not yet anyway. If a revolution overturning the ineffective and bankrupt "health care" system in the country is ever going to occur, it's going to have to start like any other life-changing revolution throughout history has—at the grass roots level. That is why I approach marketing by focusing on the individual or, for want of a better phrase, "The Little People." But hey, whatever works. If you are savvy, confident and really feel as though you can break down barriers and strongholds, go for it! Make appointments with those in charge and ask if you can present to them. You could get lucky.

What You Are Really Marketing

One more point we need to cover concerning marketing and it is perhaps the most important; you must be clear of what it is you really are marketing as a health consultant. It is not natural health, your programs, or your great products (although obviously they play a big part). It is *yourself* you are ultimately marketing, and you must always remember that fact. That means you must live the message. If someone thinks you're a phony, he/she will not sign on with you, no matter what. How would you come across as a phony? I go to numerous seminars on natural healing each year and I'm always amazed at the way some of the attending practitioners look. They're fat, have terrible skin and are out of shape. And when I go outside on breaks, some are even smoking! Now I ask, would *you* go to someone like that for advice on health? I sure wouldn't. What if you go to a fast-food place and one of your clients sees you with a soda, burger and fries? How about you're in the local eating establishment and your 1p appointment from that day sees you knocking back a margarita? What message will you be sending?

100

Practice what you preach. You are lying to your clients if you don't, and eventually it will come back to haunt you.

Another point, since you want to come across as a professional, you must look the part. Pay attention to the way you dress. I'm not implying that you go out and purchase a brand new designer wardrobe. What I am saying that you must always be aware of your public image. I sincerely hope you will never meet with clients wearing ripped up jeans, low-cut tops, tank tops, midriffs, shorts, beach apparel or sweat-suits. Nor will you ever consider attending health fairs, seminars, home-health parties or any other business-building activity dressed in such attire. Because if you do, you'll most likely be viewed as a... well, you fill in the blank. This may seem an obvious point, but I live in California and apparently, it's not. I have seen entrepreneurial and professional wannabees looking (and acting) as anything but, *especially* in the alternative health field. If you want to be taken seriously, then look the part. Cut off the dreadlocks, remove the Rastafarian hat, drop the gypsy-goddess/hippie-earth-mother get-up, get rid of the seven or eight earrings in each ear, take out the lip and/or eyebrow ring, cover up the tattoos and while you're at it, remove the amulet with the weird looking talisman from around your neck that you think wards off evil spirits. Put it in a drawer or something. And for heaven's sake, if you wear a thong, make sure the waistband isn't riding up above your trousers! Now I know what you may be thinking; "But I want to be myself! I want to be an individual!

Fine. When you're sure you are not going to run into any clients or potential clients, you can dress like Lady Gaga if you want. But for now, you may have to change your dress to what's known as *business-casual*. That means nicely pressed blouses and shirts. Well-fitting jeans, trousers, dresses and skirts. Get it? Remember, *this is not about you.* So save your "individuality" for when you're at home, or with close friends and family.

Practice Management

Aside from your knowledge of natural healing, assessment techniques, and appropriate products, effective client management will probably be your most important endeavor. How you handle your clients will either make or break your practice. This is true in all services and it is especially important in a natural health consulting business. So let's start from the beginning.

Structuring Appointments

The first appointment is perhaps your most important one. This is where you will find out the potential client's true motivation for coming to see you or to put it another way, figuring out their "why". You will ask them why they want to improve their health. They will all say they want to feel better. But you want to know *why* they want to feel better and even more important, what would their life if they *didn't* feel better. For instance, if they tell you they want to be around to see their grandchildren, ask them what it would mean if they ended up incapacitated or in a nursing home. If they want to retire and travel the world, ask them how they'd feel if they couldn't, due to a debilitating illness. You want to make this painful, encouraging them to contemplate the worst possible scenario if they don't take action *now*. Get the picture? What you're doing is showing them the problem. Then after they've realized what could happen with the dire consequences, you're going to provide the solution—*which is you. You* are going to educate them through your program as to how they can have the life in the future they want. *You* are going guide them as to how they can proceed through life with dignity, grace and vitality. If you've managed this interview correctly, they will practically be begging for your services. Does this sound manipulative? Our job is to help people avoid the medical nightmare, and chances are they will end up there if we don't help them see where they're headed! So that's the first order of business when meeting with a potential client: finding out "The Why." You'll also need to know it for when or if they're tempted to quit the program (more on that later). The next step will be to start a program that is structured and systematic. Consistency is the key to having a practice that runs smoothly. Here is one way (not the only way) to structure office visits with proven success:

First appointment: 10-12 minutes conversing with client where he/she explains health challenges and explains the "why." Remainder of time spent on assessing core issues.

Second appointment: Reviewing ROF and obtaining commitment from client towards health goals. Give him/her approximate monthly costs of supplements and appointments.

Third appointment: Present and go over tailored program, concerning supplementation, frequency of office visits, etc. NOTE: Do *not* give out your program or sell a supplement until you are sure that your client is onboard, committed and is ready to work with *you*. One reason for this is you avoid a client trying to go elsewhere to get the supplements that they could and should be purchasing from you. But also, by them getting all products from you, you also avoid him/her getting information that could be conflicting or even bad from someone else, such as a clerk in a vitamin store Another reason is you'll dispel the notion that the supplements are the program. A personally designed client-program is not just the products; it's everything; diet modification, supplements and the consultations with you.

Fourth appointment and subsequent visits thereafter: Discuss any problems/improvements and do assessment(s) to monitor progress. Fine-tune the program if necessary. Always ask how they are faring, if symptoms better, worse, etc. Sometimes they may say that they feel no improvement, yet when probed, they'll discover they've been more active, feel more energetic, have less pain, etc. At certain points in the program, it's sometimes helpful to recite verbatim the comments they wrote on their initial symptom-survey form as to how they were feeling. That will encourage clients to think about how much better they feel now as opposed to when they first came to see you.

How often you see a client is up to you. I've had people coming in as often as once or twice a week if their situation was extremely challenging. Now that may seem excessive, but it may be what's required to keep them on the program. Normally I have clients on a two-week schedule, but it depends on the situation. You want to see them in the beginning, as often as it takes to get them in full compliance to the program and are responding to it. And that might mean a couple times a week, Between the second and third appointment, I recommend as little time in between, as possible, no more than three or four days. Give them as little time as possible to change their minds. I also suggest that once they start a program, you call them within the first week to see how they are doing. If there are any problems, you'll want to address them right at the beginning. And your client will appreciate the personal phone call, something medical doctors never do.

The question may arise: how do you know when to terminate a program, meaning how do you know when a client can discontinue seeing you and stop a regimen? In every assessment system I use, there are markers for different levels of health. When the particular system(s) used registers normal, healthy, or greatly improved, the client can usually go on a maintenance program. That means discontinuing the supplements that are specifically therapeutic and reducing those that are not. It also means reducing the frequency of the visits. I do have a maintenance supplementation/office visit regimen, but it is obviously tailored to the individual. Now, if you use no assessment system other than the symptom-survey form (which I do not recommend), you're going to have to determine a suitable gauge indicating when a client can go on maintenance. Make it as definitive as you can, otherwise, you may be tempted to discontinue a program too prematurely. But I can tell you from experience that most American adults normally need to be on a structured program anywhere from three to 12 months before they can go on maintenance.

One thing you must be aware of: there will come a time when the client is tempted to quit the program. It may take a week, a month, but it will happen. It might be because they don't see results as quickly as they thought they would, or maybe their spouse is complaining about the money. It could also be because they are having trouble sticking to the program and feel that they just can't do it. Whatever the reason, you'll know when the time comes because they'll start missing appointments, complaining about money, or not refilling their supplements. When this happens you must remind them of their "Why." Repeat it back to them word for word (you should have it written down), invoking that same emotion they displayed at their first appointment. We all know how easy it is to slip away. We must help them get back on track. If they have dropped out completely and won't return your calls, you may want to do what I have done: send them an "I've Missed You" letter offering a free appointment. I want to find out why they've stopped coming and what's going on, the motive being to get them back on the program so they'll see results.

There are also instances when the client just wants to see me one time, or very infrequently. There are a number of reasons why this is so; and, what I do with these people depends on the situation. But when dealing with anyone who is interested in improving their health, my goal is to always get him/her on a structured, long-term program, because that is the only way they will experience long-lasting results. Sometimes it works and sometimes it doesn't, but I will always help someone as long as he/she is willing to stay within the guidelines of my practice. I will also sell any vitamins, minerals, and other general supplements to those who are not on a program with me. I will not however, sell products that are specifically therapeutic unless the person requesting them has been referred by another health practitioner.

Money Issues

Some clients will whine and complain about money. Although I suggest making your services as affordable as you possibly can and still stay in business (we'll discuss how later in this section), resist the urge to cave in to their whining. In the beginning, you'll probably be sympathetic when they tell you how expensive things are for them and how they really wish you took insurance. I know I was. You'll think about reducing your fees, discounting your products or even excluding products in a protocol that a client really needs. I know I did. Don't do it! If they woke up one morning and found the tires slashed on their car, they'd go out and get new ones, probably that very same day. The majority of your clients will have the money; they just have to get their priorities straight. After all, what is health worth? The way I see it, a client can pay now or pay later, meaning they'll either pay me to regain their health, or they can go their own way and eventually pay in their body. It's their choice. I am not a missionary when it comes to my practice. I spent a lot of money, time and effort to bring what I have to my community and you will too. That's not to say I have not seen clients pro-bono. I have, but it is always my decision. I will not be whined or shamed into seeing someone for free or a discounted rate. Most people wouldn't dream of asking their medical doctor for a break. Don't let them do it to you.

Here is another thing you're going to have to deal with: friends and acquaintances asking for free advice. After all, you've probably been giving it to them the whole time you've been in school. My rule of thumb is that if it something very quick, meaning if it's something I can answer in a five sentences or less, I will answer. Anything else, I will not. I will say in a very nice way, that they need to make an appointment with me. I've had friends call me and leave messages on my answering machine describing various health issues and then end with, "please call me back, as a friend." In other words, they want free. If you want to be viewed as a professional, you will need conduct yourself like one. Professionals don't do free. And besides, very few people value anything they get for nothing. If it costs nothing then to most people it's worth nothing. And besides, paying is part of the commitment.

Another item to know is that you should not overload clients with several hundred dollars worth of supplements. My comfort level on that issue is about five to seven different products per client, for a couple of reasons. The first is obviously the cost factor, but I also know that most people have an aversion to taking lots of pills and supplements in general. And they certainly don't like a program that's overly complicated. The more supplements and the more complex the program, the more likely they are to quit. It is true, most people are so malnourished and deficient, you could literally give them 20 different products and it might not be enough. Nevertheless, you must keep the plan as simple and as pared-down as you can. You do want to give them what they need so they'll get results, but don't go overboard. I also suggest only selling them enough products to get them to the next visit, unless it's a product they will be taking long-term and can save money by purchasing it in a larger size. Otherwise, sell them what they need until the next visit and nothing more.

Making it Affordable

A way to help clients (and yourself) financially is to offer a package where they pay in advance. I give a substantial discount for payment of ten to twenty appointments up-front with a clause that they must come in at least once every three weeks: otherwise all visits past and future will be prorated back to the non-discounted rate. I also tell them that all appointments must be used within a certain amount of time. In other words, they can't spread ten appointments over two years. This system works for everyone. The client receives a discounted rate and is motivated to continue seeing me as he/she has already paid in advance, and I get some up-front cash. FYI, some medical doctors and chiropractors are using a system similar to this, so fed up are they with the insurance game. Some charge a yearly fee to be paid in a lump sum allowing patients to come in as many times as they want for the twelve-month period. That may also be something for you to consider.

I always offer incentives for my established clients who help build my practice. To me, a word-of-mouth referral is the highest compliment a client can pay me, so I want to encourage and reward the person who did the referring. I do so with a program called "Health Bucks" and here's how it works: for every new client an existing client refers, I give him/her a "Health Buck" certificate worth seven dollars. Health Bucks look like play money only they have my name and address, the monetary amount and a statement saying they can be transferred, given away and/or redeemed for my services and products. I number them and keep a log of every one that goes out, and check it off when it is redeemed. People have come in with three or four at one time and they love them! I also give a discount to the new client as well, so everybody wins.

How to Price Your Services

As natural health educators, we truly are underpaid for our services. Sometimes when I think about that, I almost get angry. Here we have life-altering information, yet we practically work for peanuts because our fellow citizens do not see the amazing value of what we have. But we can structure our prices where we can collect respectable fees while still making it affordable.

When deciding what to charge for your services, you need to do a couple of things. The first thing is to decide how you want to manage your appointments time-wise. Do you want them to be one-hour long, half hour appointments or 15-minutes long? I can tell you from experience that clients for the most part, are not going to want to take an hour for every appointment. On the initial consultation where you'll do all your testing they'll expect it, but they generally won't want to spend that amount of time for follow-ups. In my practice, the second usually takes a half hour, and subsequent visits after that are 15-20 minutes. I charge by the appointment and service and not by the hour (except for phone consultations — more on that later). In other words, I have a set fee for the initial appointment and for successive office visits. The second consultation, which always consists of reviewing the ROF, is included with the initial consultation fee. I do however, have separate pricing for other services and tests that are not part of my normal appointment structure.

This model has worked for me quite well. As for other reasons for my time limits, I can also tell you that people do not want to be overloaded with information that can take time to explain. When I first started consulting, I'd go on and on with facts, figures and other information, oblivious to the "deer in the headlights" looks I'd get. I did this because I thought clients wanted it. Turns out, they didn't. What they wanted was info pertinent to their situation, not a college lecture. When clients ask, "How does this work?" what they really want to know is "*does* this work?" Your answer is, "really well!" Now on the flip side, some people will sit down with you and want to talk for an hour. And you may be tempted to let them do so, because you're too polite to tell them to zip-it. Establish right from the beginning that you're there to discuss the business at hand; the client's health challenges, the solutions and any progress. Not that you can't let them explain their situation. You can and must as the client needs to be heard. Just keep it relevant, short and no chitchat. That way, neither one of you will waste each others time. And whatever you do, don't start talking about yourself, and what you like, your experiences; unless it directly relates to them. This appointment is for them, not you.

I do understand that our goal is to educate and guide our clients. With that in mind, there are some great books out there outlining the basics of natural health. Mary Frost has written an excellent one entitled, *Going Back to the Basics of Human Health.* Get some for your office and have your clients purchase a copy at the beginning of the program, making it required reading. You can also provide handouts on subjects relevant to holistic health. That way you won't spend time during appointments talking about what they can read about on their own.

Another note of interest concerning time duration for visits; marketing studies have shown that when appointments go over 20 minutes (follow-up visits), credibility for the practitioner goes down. I'm not sure why that is, but I suspect it has to do with medical practitioners. Their appointments almost never go over 20 minutes. You as an alternative health practitioner are going to be compared to one in the medical field. You may not like it, but that's the way it is. I strongly you suggest you keep your follow up visits within that 20 minute time frame.

The second thing you need to do is to find out what would be feasible for you to charge, reasonable for the area you live in. If you live in rural Maine, you're obviously not going to be able to command the same fees as a practitioner in Beverly Hills, so you need to find out what the market will bear where you live. I also suggest researching other natural health consultants in the area (if any) that offer similar services to yours and find out what they charge. Unless they are totally unreasonable, you probably don't want to be too far off unless you have assessment devices you've paid a lot of money for. And even if you do, you're still going to have to price your services in accordance with your economic environment. The going rate in New York City is obviously going to be less than it is in Omaha. It just depends on where you live. Don't over-price yourself, but don't under-price yourself either. If your fees are too low, people will think you're second-rate.

Phone Consultations

Phone consultations for distance clients are a viable and effective way for you to help people. Some practitioners only do phone consultations. I personally like to see a client in the flesh if I'm going to help them, but sometimes that's not possible (you may want to think about using the Internet service Skype, allowing you to at least see the person, even if only by via computer). When consulting long distance, you will of course, not be able to use assessment devices where the person has to physically be in the office. But you can use other methods, such as urine testing, saliva testing or hair analysis and the required symptom survey. Consulting via phone will not be too much different from consulting with non-distance clients. You will still get all the necessary forms, including authorization and health questionnaire (either by fax or email). On the initial call, you will always get their "why" and try to decipher the core issues. The second call or appointment will be reviewing the ROF, and on the third, you will explain the program. The fourth, fifth and so on will be as outlined in the previous section. As far as supplements go, you can have products drop-shipped after you've received payment, but just be sure that your supplement company will send the bill to you and not to the client. Your clients will not be happy believe me, if they see what *you* pay for supplements versus what they pay!

As far as pricing goes, I quote an hourly rate as the initial charge, not including any tests that have to be mailed out. For those I charge the going rate along with postage. The second appointment is a half hour, so I charge half my hourly rate. If they go over the half hour (by their request) I charge in 15-minute increments. All appointments after the second are 20 minutes and I charge one-third the hourly rate. As far as payment goes, I always obtain the credit card number information (you'll need to secure a service) *before* the call unless they have paid for a block of appointments. One more thing about phone consults worth mentioning: don't be tempted to think that just because your consultation is by phone, you should be charging less. You are dispensing life-changing information regardless of how it's delivered.

Problem Solving

Most practitioners just starting out feel like they must take anyone who walks through the door. You don't have to, nor should you. In fact, the wrong client can actually hurt your practice. Most of the people I've consulted with have been wonderful, but I've had a few who have drained my energy and eroded my confidence. I call them *psychic vampires*. The money I received from these individuals was not worth the aggravation, so now I screen everyone right from the beginning. Before I work with anyone, they must meet *my* standards. That means it's *my way or the highway*. That may sound tough, but I only want to work with people who are truly committed to changing their health. Not everyone is, even though they will solicit your services. The challenge is figuring out who is serious and who is not.

Unsuitable Clients

I once had a client who, every time she walked in my door, would start complaining. She complained about everything, how awful she always felt, how awful her friends were, how awful life was and on and on. In addition, she would challenge me on everything, her protocol, her progress, my testing, etc. It got to the point that whenever I'd see her name on the schedule, I'd get that sinking feeling in my stomach. It all came to a head when on one visit she started her usual complaining. Only this time I'd had enough. I calmly and quietly informed her that it would greatly benefit her if she'd just change her attitude. I told her she needed to have a positive, thankful attitude and to start thinking about the things she could do in life instead of those she couldn't. I also made it clear that one of the reasons she wasn't progressing with her health was because of her negative outlook. She was furious. The following week I received a three-page letter she'd written, expressing how unsympathetic and insensitive she felt I was to her situation. But the last sentence was the clincher: she asked to change the day of her regular appointment! I released her (in a very professional way via snail-mail) and referred her to someone else. I realized that I could not help this woman as she really didn't want to get well. Her illness was her identity and she was just using me to show the world that I was yet another health professional that couldn't help her because she was different. So don't assume everyone who comes to see you wants what you have. You must do your best to try and weed out those who don't or they can cause big problems. If they manage to get through your screening process, get rid of them as soon as possible. If they've paid in advance for appointments, *happily* refund the balance.

As far as children go, I will take them on only if their parents will commit to a health-building program at the same time. *Because if the parents won't, the children won't.* I've also had people in my office who have been dragged in by someone else, like a spouse, family member or friend, because "they really need it." I don't usually take them on either. Even if they say they are willing to try, they usually end up quitting because they didn't want to be there in the first place. I do not try to convince anyone to change his/her health. I only want to work with those enlightened souls who truly want to change their situation *now.*

Then, there are those individuals who begin a program, but don't really understand what's involved. They may after awhile get frustrated, or even challenge the validity of a program itself. To avoid that situation, I always inform people right from the start that it will take *commitment* and *time* to change their condition, sometimes *months* — *with no discernible results.* If they gasp at that statement, I remind them that because it took however many years leading to their present situation, it's not going to change overnight. I also point out that it's going to take money for supplements and appointments. In addition, I make clear that although they don't have to give up all their offending foods and habits immediately (unless their condition warrants it), *I expect them to adhere to the program we have set out.* If they do not agree to *all* these conditions, I will *not* work with them. Now, some will agree and still not comply, or may even flat-out refuse to do what's required. I know of a practitioner who had a client with severe asthma. As milk impeded his healing progress, he needed to give it up, and he agreed to do so. After a month the practitioner was puzzled as to why he wasn't seeing any results, until the client told him he was still pouring milk on his morning oatmeal. This guy just couldn't believe that the small amount milk he was drinking was causing problems and refused to give it up. The practitioner released him and told him that if he told anyone in town that his program didn't work he'd be lying, because *he didn't stick to it.* Now that may sound combative on the part of the practitioner, but it was very wise. He knew from experience that if you let your clients get away with non-compliance, they will not see results. And if they don't see results, they will tell people that *your* programs do not work, damaging your reputation and hindering your success. Set your standards right at the beginning and stick to them.

Most people will seek your advice because they understand you're highly trained, but every once in a while I'll have someone who wants to show me how much *they* know about my chosen profession. They'll go on and on, quoting studies, books and all sorts of related factoids. This same type of client quite often feels compelled to present me with a shopping bag full of the various supplements they've been taking. I don't usually mind because I'm going to ask them to show me what they've been taking anyway. But what I *do* mind is when they come in with an unreasonable list of things they will or won't do when it comes to a program. Which is really silly, because if what they were doing were working, they wouldn't be sitting in my office in the first place! I tactfully convey this to them and usually they see the point. But if not, I won't work with them. I once had a woman who told me that she wanted to begin a program, but refused to give up her online-purchased supplements (she'd paid a lot of money for them). They were poor-quality and would obstruct any healing plan I might design. My testing confirmed this, but she still would not budge. Either she didn't believe my testing or she was unteachable. Either way, she was an unsuitable candidate for my services.

And while we're on the subject of clients and their supplements, many in the beginning are eager to show you what they believe they've been doing right. It's human nature, as we all want to be good little boys and girls. They'll show you their junky vitamins, indigestible, chemical/rock-minerals from the 99-cent store and all the other crap they're taking, thinking they've really been helping themselves. It's kind of like when a cat brings you a dead mouse. He wants you to say, "good kitty." He wants praise. It's the same with people. So I praise them for their "dead mice," telling them it's great they've been trying to improve their health. I never tell them what I really think, not at first anyway. Instead, I harness their enthusiasm, praise their efforts, and encourage them to "take it to the next level." What happens is that they almost always end up throwing out their cheapy-toxic supplements on their own, without me saying a word.

Communication/Compliance

Client compliance is probably the biggest concern among practitioners. There isn't one on the face of the earth, natural or allopathic, that hasn't had to deal with this issue. We

123

all want to become effective where client compliance is concerned ensuring positive results. So the first place to start is learning to become an effective communicator. How well you communicate will have much to do with the compliance factor. As an example, if a client tells me they've totally blown his/her program due to a party the past weekend, I do not do the "it's ok, everybody blows it" thing. My reaction is always silence. By doing that they know I am not condoning the activity, but I'm not condemning it either. I wait for them to tell me what they're going to do next and then respond accordingly. If you let them get away with unproductive behavior, you will not be helping them.

And here's a crucial truth on compliance that's often overlooked as it's metaphysical—your clients will never be more compliant than you are. I have seen this repeatedly, not just in my practice, but with others as well. If you eat processed sugar but espouse eliminating it, guess what: your clients won't do it no matter what you say. You want them to exercise but you don't? They won't do that either. So, walk the talk. You'll not only be helping your clients, you'll be helping yourself as well, knowing and feeling the results of an honest life.

The Gradient Factor

When dealing with clients, a*lways work with them using gradient steps*. When you're a new practitioner, your inclination might be to tell your clients to give up everything at once, all the sugar, caffeine, white flour, alcohol, everything, and adopt a complete change of diet and lifestyle in one fell swoop. You do that and chances are you'll lose them, in one fell swoop. This is rule number one as to what *not* to do with a new client: *never, ever* tell your him/her to give up everything at once. So many beginning practitioners do this and it just isn't feasible, as most people wouldn't be able to handle such a dramatic change even if they wanted to do it. First, if they have family members who are not supportive they'll probably get flack or ridicule—not an encouraging situation. Secondly, they will experience a healing crisis and the more toxic they are, the worse it will be. And you know what that means; headaches, fatigue, cravings, even nausea. Not a good thing if you're trying to do the things we all have to do, like work, take care of our families and maintain relationships. We always want to work in steps. For example, if you have someone who is drinking 20 diet sodas a week, for the first week of the program have him/her commit to having 18. The following week, have them drink 15, the next week 10 and so on. They will still feel better and the healing reaction will be kept to a minimum, making it easier for them to stick to the regimen.

Never Do This

Item number two that you must never do, and that is suggest to a brand new client that he/she have all their silver fillings removed. Now I am well aware of the amalgam issue, but here's what can happen. First, as filling removal is costly, clients will see it as an added, mandatory expense to your program. Remember, they're most likely already seeing your program as an out-of-pocket financial burden, so you don't want to make it even more expensive. Second, you'll be associated with dentistry and you don't want that. I don't know anyone who likes going to the dentist. You want your clients to look forward to their visits and they won't if every time they see you, they think, oh, I've got to go to the dentist...And third and probably most important, the removal of amalgams can make a person worse if they're not physically ready (if the client is coming to see you specifically for filling-removal-preparation, that's different). You can cause a person some major physical stress if fillings are removed before his/her body can handle it. Now granted, many of my clients in the beginning do ask about their fillings. But they literally breathe a sigh of relief when I tell them that we can talk about it down the road! So, I wait a while before the subject comes up and I'll only mention it when I know a client really trusts me, and/or when I feel he/she can handle it.

No-shows

Another issue to think about as a practitioner is what to do when clients no-show, or do not give 24 hours notice. Now, maybe you won't care when it happens—and it will—and you're cool enough about things like that to let them slide. I'm not. Here's what happens when they do it a second time (they get one "freebie"): I either charge a fee equal to one appointment, which I donate to a local charity enabling the client to write it off, or I deduct an appointment if they have paid in advance. If they have the prepaid plan they can choose the penalty. I do, however, call everyone the day before confirming the appointment time. If they still no-show, the fee stands. This lets them know I am serious about what I do and value my time as much as they value theirs. Fortunately, this hasn't happened too often. But I let them know on my forms, which they are required to sign, my policy on no-showing for a scheduled appointment.

Some Will, Some Won't, So What

You should be aware that even if you've done all you can do to be as client-friendly as possible, some are going to flake no matter what. I've had clients happily agree to everything we set out, seem very excited, even pay for ten appointments at once and not come to one of them. I'd call them trying to find out why, with no response. I used to take it personally, but I got over it. Don't get discouraged. Just carry on and have the "SWSWSW" attitude — *"some will, some won't, so what."*

Deciding What Products to Use

The type of products you use will be a matter of preference and will depend on your personal philosophy. For example, if you are hard-over on veganism, you will not want products that have animal products. If you're committed to having only products that are entirely made up of whole-food, you will not want those with any synthetics. But whatever line(s) you choose, be sure the company has good customer service *and* some sort of system as to how to train practitioners to use them. Many supplement companies offer DVDs, seminars, and local study groups. Some companies use webinars, email and calls to get their info out. Taking advantage of these resources is crucial to your success, as they will increase your base of knowledge along with your confidence. Tap into as many of them as you possibly can.

I have two main lines in my practice and carry a few products of some others as well. No company has the best products for every situation, no matter what they claim. It is more expensive to carry numerous lines, but you will have better results. I have some favorites, which are listed in the appendix with contact information. You can check them out yourself.

Carrying Network Marketing Products

Many natural health practitioners carry multi-level or network-marketing products in their offices. If you aren't familiar with the business model of networking marketing companies, you will be very soon. When word gets out as to what you do, someone will be calling on you, wanting you to distribute products from one of the hundreds of companies out there. The way it works is this: you sign on with a company to carry or use a product by becoming a distributor. When those you introduce to the products buy them, you get a commission. When those people find other people to buy the products, you get a commission from those sales as well. Then when those people buy products, you get paid, and so on and so forth.

It can be very lucrative as the income potential can be almost limitless, but there are issues you must be aware of. First, the retail mark-up is normally very low, so if you want to earn a substantial income you will have to build a business. That means having people who order the products on a regular basis *and* finding people who want to distribute them as well. Your first inclination might be to tap into your client base. Some practitioners do this, but you must be very, very careful. If your clients think you are using them to build a business, they may feel that their trust is being violated and question your loyalties. Are you recommending a product that's not necessary, but would benefit *you* financially? If they think that's the case, they'll tell their friends, family and business associates, damaging your reputation.

I am a big proponent of having multiple streams of revenue, especially where residual/passive income is concerned.

But the hard, cold fact is that starting out as a new practitioner building a practice, *and* building a lucrative network marketing business at the same time is almost impossible. Yes, I know, I've been to the MLM meetings where they'll show a chiropractor, dentist or maybe a real estate agent who has made big bucks in the business while working in their professions. And they tell you than you can too. But notice that none of these people they will present are neophytes. They've almost always been at their practices/professions a long time and are well established. Being a successful network marketer takes a lot of time and hard work. Building any business takes a lot of time and hard work, especially in the beginning. If you truly want a thriving practice you will need to be focused and driven. Trying to build a network marketing business while starting your practice will be a major distraction. Set your goals as to where you want to be in your natural health consulting business and stick to them. Don't let anyone or anything slow you down.

Deciphering Online Information

No one would argue that the Internet has been key to the proliferation of information on health. According to a recent poll, it was estimated that over 90 million people searched the web for health information in 2008. And while that is a good thing, just remember that *anyone* can post a site saying *anything* they want. So whom can you trust? The first rule is to know where the information is coming from. Look for a reliable source such as a well-known medical or naturopathic/natural health school, medical association, health-care institution, or national disease-centered organization. Beware of .com (commercial) sites as they usually are trying to sell something. Some can have valuable information, but if they start making outlandish claims about their products with only testimonies and anecdotal information to back them up, a red flag should go up

One site to stay away from is *Quackwatch*. This site for years has put out inflammatory and misleading information aimed at completely discrediting the natural health movement and anyone associated with it. It has discouraged many new natural health practitioners until they realize that the writer(s) is a moron when it comes to nutrition, and health in general. One wonders about the author's motivation. I'm not about to speculate as to what it is here, but suffice to say it is not to add to the helpful-health knowledge of the USA! So, stay clear. Below are some sites for you to investigate:

lifestylemanagement.com/licensure_laws.htm - *Site giving info on state-by-state licensing laws concerning dietetics and nutrition (biased against unlicensed consultants, so be discerning)*

behealthyatwork.com - *Great site offering health info concerning the workplace.*

coryholly.com – *Site offering online sports and fitness education programs from a holistic viewpoint*

westonaprice.org/ - *The Weston A. Price Foundation site*

ppnf.org/catalog/ppnf/ - *Price-Pottenger Nutritional Information*

mercola.com/ - *Dr. Mercola's website on natural health, the most visited site concerning health on the Internet*

wholehealthmd.com - *Vitamin therapies for various health challenges. Also includes recipes and links to natural health shopping sites*

alternativemedicine.com- *Research and articles from Alternative Medicine Magazine*

purefood.org- *Articles on organic food and the problems with our present food supply*

health.org/index - *Site concerning substance abuse.*

familyvillage.wisc.edu - *For children with special health needs.*

babycenter.com - *Information on pregnancy and pediatrics.*

hacres.com - *Site based on Biblical health principles, espousing the vegan diet.*

webmd.com - *Health information site for professionals and laypeople.*

alzheimers.com -*News, advice and new treatment info.*

cmch.com/mhn - *Site on mental health.*

safewireless.org- *Info on dangers of cell phones and wireless technology.*

informedbeauty.com - *Site on beauty from the inside out.*

earthclinic.com- *Folk remedies from around the world.*

truehealthfacts.com- *ranked number one alternative site on degenerative diseases.*

Personal Development

What can I say about personal development other than as human beings we should seek to attain the highest level of it that we possibly can? We must always strive to be better servants and leaders. We must focus on the needs of others, truly listening to what they are telling us. Isn't it amazing how so few people know how to listen? When someone is speaking are you listening to what they're saying or are you already planning on what you will say next? When you carry on a conversation with someone, are you listening to his opinion or are you too busy expressing yours? Are you interested in other people or are you trying to be interesting? Here's a tip: people will love you if you shut your mouth and let them talk! Really, they will. Think about it. Of the people to whom you are really drawn, what is their most compelling trait? Is their good looks or stunning intellect? Probably not. Most likely it's their ability to quietly listen, a quality so lacking in this loud and graceless age. When I was younger, I used to admire intelligence. Now I admire kindness, and a kind person always listens.

So, take a good, hard look at yourself and be honest as to where you need improvement. We all need it and as a leader — which is what you are as a natural health consultant — self-development must be a priority. People will be looking to you for help and guidance. Leaders help people get what they want, and if you help enough people get what they want, you'll get what you want. It is your joyful obligation to be the best you can be. There is a plethora of programs to help you: Jim Roan, Tony Robbins and Dale Carnegie are just a few Yes, it will cost you some money, but it will be one of the best investments you will ever make.

Closing Thoughts

These are the basics as to what you will need to start a nutritional consulting business. However, I couldn't end this guide without pointing out that as an alternative health practitioner, you will face resistance. Maybe you've felt it already. It is true; we have made great strides when it comes to acceptance in our field. But to most of mainstream American, we're still fringe. You're going to get opposition, so be prepared. It may come from family members, friends or business associates, or sadly, even within the alternative health field itself. As I write this, there is a battle going on against the unlicensed natural health practitioner, primarily perpetrated by the naturopathic medical schools. They are hell-bent on degrading and discrediting traditional naturopathy, which is amazing as this hybrid breed between drug doctors and natural health practitioners — which is what naturopathic physicians are — didn't even exist until recently. Graduates of these schools are brainwashed into believing that they are real naturopaths because they've had medical diagnostic training. So much for the thousands of years of healing by Native Americans, Asian Cultures, Eastern Indians and all the other systems that have been around for eons. But don't let it get to you. Ignore the politics. But if you do start feeling discouraged, just remember: it's not about you. It's about a lost and suffering nation dying for help. Think of yourself as a conduit of hope. Picture yourself as a life raft. You offer something this country desperately needs — a light in the darkness.

Find someone who really believes in you and will help you get started. That could be your parents, sibling, spouse, friend, anyone who will be there for you. Don't forget, in the beginning you're not just going to be the health guru, you're going to be handling accounting, marketing, scheduling, inventory, all of it; so don't be afraid to ask for help. When I first started I had my husband to help me, but things really got going when I took on an apprentice, a natural health student who lived locally. It was a great situation for both of us. She has since moved to another state where she has started her own practice, but I take great pride in the fact that I helped launch her career!

Other suggestions: be humble and teachable. Along with school and seminars, you will probably learn the most from your clients. They have a lot to teach you, so listen. And lastly, don't be too hard on yourself. In the beginning, you will make mistakes. Honor the learning curve. Like any new endeavor, you cannot expect to have everything down in the beginning. But where your clients are concerned, always know that they are better for seeing you than if they never saw you at all, *even if your program is not perfect*. Anything you do will almost always help them, and you sure as heck can't say that about the medical profession! You have taken on one of the noblest undertakings there can ever be; helping to put an end to human suffering. So go out and do the thing you were born to do. May God bless you in your efforts.

Appendix-Sample Forms and Lists

Kay K. Larson, Ph.D., Naturopathic Consultant

AUTHORIZATION FORM

I, _____, in affixing my signature to
this instrument do thereby agree to and understand the following:

1. That Kay K. Larson, is a natural health counselor who is legally able to instruct and educate others in self-help methods of health such as the use of proper exercise, diet, nutritional supplements, water, sunshine, fresh air, rest and attitude;

2. That Kay K. Larson, in no context of the phrase "practices medicine" and therefore does not diagnose, prescribe, treat, administer, cure, heal or otherwise perform a duty that is reserved for those who are licensed to do so;

3. That the instruction concerning a healthful lifestyle is incidental to any particular illnesses and diseases I may have and is therefore not made in direct references to these;

4. Any healing of illnesses or diseases I may experience as a result of following the instruction of Kay K. Larson, was purely the result of the body itself once a naturally correct way of living was employed, for it is only the body that heals itself, not any person;

5. That no claims or guarantees have been made as to any health benefits that may result from my following the instruction given by Kay K. Larson, concerning a naturally correct way of living;

6. That the instruction given by Kay K. Larson, in no way replaces proper medical care, and that I am free to choose a naturally right lifestyle;

7. That under penalty of perjury I am not an agent of any branch of the federal, state or local government for any agency thereof, with intent to entrap or entice Kay K. Larson, her staff, employees and/or associates into breaking any federal, state, or local law whatsoever, acting either on my own behalf or on behalf of the agency of the government or on behalf of any government agency directly;

Signed_____

Date _____

PERMISSION & AUTHORIZATION FORM REGARDING THE USE OF NUTRITIONAL DETERMINATION TESTING
PLEASE READ BEFORE SIGNING

I specifically authorize Kay K. Larson, Ph.D., a non-licensed Naturopathic Consultant, to perform nutritional determination testing to develop a natural complementary health improvement program for me that may include dietary guidelines, nutritional supplements, etc., in order to assist me in improving my health **and not for the treatment or "cure" of any disease.**

I understand that nutritional determination testing is safe, non-invasive and uses natural methods of analyzing the body's physical and nutritional needs, and that deficiencies or imbalance in these areas could cause or contribute to various health problems.

I understand that nutritional determination testing are not methods for "diagnosing" or the "treatment" of any disease or medical condition.

No promise or guarantee has been made regarding the results any tests or any natural health, nutritional or dietary programs recommended, but rather I understand that these tests are ways by which the body's responses can be used as an aid to determine possible nutritional imbalances, so that safe, natural programs can be developed for the purpose of bringing about a better state of health.

I have read and understand the foregoing

This permission form applies to subsequent visits and consultations.

Print Name_____

Address_____

City_____ State_____ Zip Code_____

Phone_____

Signed_____ Date_____
(If minor, signature of parent or guardian required)

144

Family History

Do you have a family history of any of the following, including parents, siblings, children and spouse?

Cancer	Y	N	Who? _____
Diabetes	Y	N	Who? _____
Heart Disease	Y	N	Who? _____
Hepatitis	Y	N	Who? _____
High Blood Pressure	Y	N	Who? _____
Stroke	Y	N	Who? _____
Epilepsy	Y	N	Who? _____
Mental Illness	Y	N	Who? _____
Asthma	Y	N	Who? _____
Kidney Disease	Y	N	Who? _____
Glaucoma	Y	N	Who? _____
Tuberculosis	Y	N	Who? _____

Please Circle   Yes or No

Scarlet Fever	Y N	Diphtheria	Y N	Rheumatic Fever	Y N
Mumps	Y N	Measles	Y N	German measles	Y N

What hospitalizations or surgeries have you had?

_____

X-rays, CAT scans, MRIs have you had_____
Electrocardiogram Y N   Electroencephalogram Y N

Immunizations:

Polio   Y N   Tetanus shot Y N   Measles/Mumps/Rubella Y N
Small Pox   Y N
Other_____

Please list any knows allergens, food, drugs or other_____

Please list your health concerns as to why you are here and what you'd like help with:

_____
_____
_____
_____
_____
_____
_____

Client Information

Name _____ Age _____ Date _____

Phone _____ Date of birth _____

Email address _____

Occupation _____

Who referred you? _____

When and Where did you last receive medical care? _____

For what reason? _____

Why are you here today? _____

_____

Please list any and all medications you are taking, including painkillers, laxatives,
and vitamins and other supplements: _____

_____

_____

Please list your general diet for **most of your life:** (be truthful!)

Breakfast _____

Lunch _____

Dinner _____

Snacks _____

Do you eat:	Often	Sometimes	Never		Often	Sometimes	Never
Eggs				Fruits			
Meat				Salads			
Chicken				Cooked Veg.			
Fish				Cofee			
Milk				Potatoes			
Cheese				Rice			
Butter				Pasta			
Yogurt				Breads			
Sugar				Salt			

Would you say you eat a lot of junk food? Y N

If you drink coffee, how many cups per day? _____

Do you smoke? Y N Do you crave sweets? Y N Chocolate? Y N

Do you drink alcohol? Y N. If yes, how many drinks per week? _____

How do you sleep? _____ Energy level: 1-2-3-4-5-6-7-8-9-10 **(1=lowest, 10=highest)**

Do you have bowel distress such as gas, pain or constipation? **Never Sometimes Always**

Do you eat sushi? (raw fish) Y N If yes, how often? _____

Do you have pets? Y N

Do you exercise? Y N Type_____ How many times a week_____

How many glasses of water do you drink a day? _____

Have you had any major emotional traumas that you feel have affected your health? Y N

Symptom Survey

Name _____ Date: _____

Telephone (Cell) _____ (Home) _____ (Work) _____

Street Address _____

Street Address _____

City _____ State _____ Zip _____

Age _____ Weight _____ Height _____ Gender _____

Marital Status _____

Occupation _____

INSTRUCTIONS: Place number next to issue that applies to you.

Use (1) for mild symptoms/frequency, (2) for moderate, and (3) for severe.

Group 1
_____ Acid foods upset
_____ Get chilled Often
_____ Lump in throat
_____ Dry mouth-eyes-nose
_____ Pulse speeds after meals
_____ Keyed up-hard to calm down
_____ Cuts heal slowly
_____ Gag easily
_____ Unable to relax/easily startled
_____ Sensitive to Bright Lights
_____ Uuine amount smaller than usual
_____ nervous stomach
_____ Appetite reduced
_____ Has cold sweats
_____ Often has fevers
_____ Shooting pains in face
_____ Do not blink often
_____ Sour Stomach

Group 2
_____ Joint stifness after arising
_____ Muscle-leg/toe cramps at night
_____ Often cold
_____ Eyes or nose watery
_____ Blink often
_____ Swollen/puffy eyes
_____ Indigestion after meals
_____ Always hungry/lightheaded
_____ Vomiting frequently
_____ Perspire easily
_____ Breathing irregular
_____ Pulse slow/irregular
_____ Difficulty swollowing
_____ Poor circulation

Group 3
_____ Eat when nervous
_____ Excessive appetite
_____ Always hungry
_____ Shaky when hungry
_____ Always hungry
_____ Afternoon headaches
_____ Crave candy/coffee in afternoon
_____ Wake after a few hours of sleep
_____ Mood swings/depression
_____ Heart palpitates if meal missed or delayed
_____ High cravings for sweets/breads/snacks
_____ Mood swings/depression
_____ Heart palpitates if meal missed or delayed
_____ High cravings for sweets/breads/snacks

Group 4
_____ Hands and feet go to sleep easily
_____ Sighs freqiently
_____ Susceptive to colds and fevers
_____ Swollen ankles worse at night
_____ Muscle Cramps
_____ Bruise Easily
_____ Frequent nose bleeds
_____ Noise in head or ringing in ears

Group 5
_____ Dizziness
_____ Dry Skin
_____ Burning Feet
_____ Itchy skin and feet
_____ Excessive hair fallout
_____ Frequent skin rashes
_____ Metalic/bitter taste in mornings
_____ Bowel movements painful/difficult
_____ Worries a lot
_____ Pain between shoulder blades
_____ Bad breath
_____ Burning or itching anus
_____ Greasy food upset
_____ Sneezing attacks

Group 6
_____ Lower bowel gas hours after eating
_____ Burning stomach relieved by eating
_____ Coated Tongue
_____ Pass large amounts foul smelling gas
_____ Bloated stomach after eating
_____ Loss of taste for meat
_____ Gas hortly after sater
_____ Gas 1/2-3 hours after eating
_____ Mucus colitis or irritable bowel

Group 7
_____ Insomnia
_____ Nervousness
_____ Can'r gain weight-increased appetite
_____ Intolerance to heat
_____ Highly emotional
_____ Night Sweats
_____ Irritable and restless
_____ Eyelid and facial twitch
_____ Pulse fast at rest
_____ Weight gain
_____ Tire easily
_____ Sensitive to cold
_____ Hair course, falls out
_____ Dry or scaly skin

_____ Increased sex drive
_____ Headaches, splitting
_____ decreased sugar tolerance
_____ abnormal thirst
_____ weight gain around hips or waist
_____ reduced or no sex drive
_____ menstrual disorders
_____ lack of menstruation (young girls)
_____ hot flashes
_____ Weakness, fatigue
_____ Nails break easily
_____ hives, itchy skin
_____ Respritory problems
_____ Swollen ankles
_____ Salt cravinns

Female Only:
_____ Very Easily fatigues
_____ Premenstrual tension
_____ Painful breats
_____ Acne,worses at menses
_____ Long term depression
_____ Depressed before menstruation
_____ hot flashes
_____ Vaginal Discharge
_____ Menses light or missed
_____ Hysterectomy/ovaries removed

Male Only
_____ Prostate Only
_____ Urination difficult or dribling
_____ Frequent night urination
_____ Depression
_____ Pain on inside of legs or heels
_____ Feeling of incomplete bowel movement
_____ Tire easily
_____ Diminished sex drive
_____ Restless Legs at night

List Three Main Health Concerns:

_____

_____

_____

_____

_____

NUTRITIONAL PROGRAM

Client Name_____   Date_____

Take for _____

SUPPLEMENT	INSTRUCTIONS

Special Instructions:

POST ON YOUR REFRIGERATOR

Kay K. Larson PhD

148

Distance/Online Natural Health and Nutrition Schools

American College of Health Care Sciences (USDE accredited)
achs.edu

Everglades University (USDE accredited)
evergladesuniversity.edu/bachelor_degree1.htm

Global College of Natural Medicine
gcnm.com/

Hawthorn University
hawthornuniversity.org/Home.aspx

Huntington College of Health Sciences
hchs.edu/

Institute for Integrative Nutrition
integrativenutrition.com/

Kingdom College of Natural Health
kcnh.org/

Natural Healing College
naturalhealingcollege.com/

Natural Healing Institute
naturalhealinginst.com/

New Eden School of Natural Health and Herbal Studies
newedenschool.webs.com/

Trinity College of Natural Health
trinityschool.org/

University of Bridgeport (USDE Accredited)
bridgeport.edu/pages/2272.asp

University of Natural Health
unh-edu.org/

University of Natural Medicine
universitynaturalmedicine.org/

Westbrook University
westbrooku.edu/index.htm

Assessment Systems:

Asyra (BioEnegetic Testing)
asyra.com

BioMeridian Inc. (Electro-Dermal Screening)
biomeridian.com/

Hair Analysis Kit (Mineral Check)
vivagen.net/tests_distillers.htm

Heart Rate Variable Testing
nerveexpress.com/

Metabolic Urinalysis
Email: terrainmed@aol.com

Metemetrix Labs
metametrix.com

Nuritional Response Testing (Deltoid Muscle Testing)
unsinc.info/aboutus.html

Sclerology (Sclera Analysis)
sclerology-institute.org/sclerologist.htm

VoiceBio™© (Voice Analysis)
voicebio.com/

Supplement and Health Product Companies:

Apex Energetics, CA
apexenergetics.com/

BioGenesis Nutraceuticals, WA
bio-genesis.com/index.html

Deseret Biologicals
desbio.com/

Designs for Health, CT
designsforhealth.com

Doctor's Research, CA
doctorsresearch.com/

Inno-Vita, UT
inno-vita.com

Newton Homeopathics, GA
newtonlabs.net/

Malpractice Insurance:

Granite State Insurance Company
Authorized Representative: CM&F Group Inc.
800-221-4904 or 212-233-8940

Marsh Insurance Company
(Underwritten by the Affinity group)
800-503-9230

Health Insurance for Small Business Owners:

Health Care Providers Service Organization
http://www.hpso.com/

Assurant Health
Assuranthealth.com/corp/ah/healthplans/major-medical.htm